THE REDEEMING CHRIST

The Redeeming Christ

PETER J. RIGA

CORPUS BOOKS: *WASHINGTON & CLEVELAND*

CORPUS PUBLICATIONS

EDITORIAL OFFICES: 1330 Massachusetts Ave., N.W.
Washington, D.C. 20005

SALES & DISTRIBUTION: 2231 West 110th Street
Cleveland, Ohio 44102

Library of Congress Catalog Card Number: 79-83514

DESIGN BY LA LIBERTÉ & RAYNER

FIRST PRINTING 1969

Printed in the United States of America

For the Innocent Children of Biafra
In My Pain for Their Suffering

"And he . . . began to be greatly distressed and troubled. . . . 'Abba, Father, all things are possible to thee; remove this cup from me; yet not what I will, but what thou wilt'"

MARK 14:33, 36

Table of Contents

Introduction

The heart of the Christian message is that Jesus, the Son of God, died and rose from the dead, thereby accomplishing the salvation of all men from the death of sin. This message became the whole preaching of the primitive Christian and apostolic community and, consequently, became the focal point of the Gospels themselves. It is very clear that this message was first preached by the disciples of Jesus as *the* good news of salvation to all men and was only later codified in written documents. The influence of this preaching can be found throughout the Gospel narratives of the passion and resurrection of the Savior.

The whole of Christianity falls or rises on this central teaching of faith: Jesus is risen and is now the Lord of all creation. The first disciples of Jesus preached it as a simple fact to be accepted or rejected by the hearers of the Word. It is this same message which was written in the texts that have come down to us with that same witness. Indeed, this same witness alone constitutes the mission of the Church and all Christians. This preaching is the same today as it was from the mouths of the apostles themselves. The totality of the Christian reality depends upon this important fact. It is not something which can be proved as a historical fact as such, since the resurrection, although historic, was not historical. It was a unique and irreducible fact which formed the essence of the Christian message, liturgy, and economy.

In the following pages we have attempted to clarify and explain the precise meaning of the written accounts of these events which are contained in the New Testament, particularly in the Gospels.* The following is not meant to be a line by line commentary. Its purpose entails providing a general explanation for use by the faithful Christian so that he may achieve a more profound understanding of what constitutes the essence of his faith. If it manages to do this, the effort of this book will have been worthwhile. The Gospels proposed the fact of the death and resurrection of Jesus to those who had faith. Those who read these pages will find only a witness of faith, not rational proof. In all honesty, the fact of the death and resurrection of Jesus cannot be proved regardless of how much authentic circumstantial evidence is brought forth. In the final analysis, belief in this truth of faith is precisely a grace of God, and no effort is made here to show how "reasonable" the resurrection really was. It was not reasonable at all, for it was contrary to all laws of history and probability. This is usually the way of God with men. His ways are not man's ways; he responds to man in ways which man can neither comprehend nor rationalize; he must simply accept as a child accepts the love of his Father. When all is said and done, God's response of love for men in the death and resurrection of Jesus simply goes beyond the human categories of beauty and awe: one can only worship and give thanks.

PETER J. RIGA

THE REDEEMING CHRIST

I

The Passion Narratives

The canonical (inspired) sources of the passion, death, and resurrection of Jesus contain the very core of the good news of salvation. It is no surprise that the primitive Christian community established its whole teaching around this theme; consequently, when the accounts of our Gospels were actually written (between 50 and 100 A.D.), they became the most developed and most detailed parts of the written Gospels.

The canonical sources of the passion-death-resurrection of Jesus include the Acts of the Apostles. This is important, because the Acts is a record of the first preaching of the good news of salvation which resided precisely in the fact of the death-resurrection of Jesus. The passion of Jesus was an essential part of that message and was necessarily included within it.

The most detailed sources of our knowledge of the passion of Jesus are the four Gospels (Mt 26:1; Mk 14:1; Lk 22:1; Jn 11:47). In a strict sense the passion cycle begins with the agony of Gethsemane and concludes with the burial of Jesus. Yet we shall consider the passion accounts in a broader sense, namely, as encompassing the events preceding the Gethsemane scene and the post-passion events, including the resurrection of Jesus.

There are many detailed aspects recounted for us in the passion narratives: the conspiracy against the life of Jesus, the anointing at Bethany, the betrayal by Judas, the Paschal meal

1

and announcement of the betrayal, the agony in the garden (not found in St. John), the arrest in the garden, the trial of Jesus, the denial of Peter connected with the trial, the Sanhedrin's condemnation, the mockery and beating by the Jewish soldiers, the turning over of the prisoner to Roman authorities, the trial before Pilate, the episode of Barabbas, the flagellation, the condemnation to death, the march from Jerusalem to Calvary, the arrival and crucifixion, the death of Jesus, and his burial. These events bring out two rather strong points.

The first point is that the account of the passion of Jesus is more developed than the rest of the Gospel, which is general and schematic. The passion events occurred in only a few hours. Therefore, it becomes immediately evident that the early Christian community kept a detailed account of these precious hours. They were regarded as being the most important in the whole life of Jesus. This explains why the passion account encompasses such a large section of the Gospels of Matthew and Mark. Nearly half of the Gospel in the account of St. John is devoted to it.

The second point is that although each evangelist has the same basic general plan, there are differences concerning details and orientation. One of the main preoccupations of the following pages will be to understand why these differences occur and to ascertain their influence on the theology of the passion.

We will follow three distinct stages in the study of the passion narratives. We will first offer a literary analysis of the texts; next, a historical criticism of these same sources; and finally, an attempt to find their religious significance.

Literary Analysis of the Passion Narratives

Scripture scholars have investigated the passion narratives in the past fifty years, and two main problems have appeared. The first is that we must find out whether it is possible to find in the Gospel of Mark, which scholars agree is the most ancient

Gospel, a primitive tradition which is also used in the other Gospels. Second, we must attempt to find the particular literary form, if one exists, used in the passion narratives.

The first question is very difficult to answer. It relies on the scholarly study of the various literary forms used in the composition of the passion narratives. This is difficult, because the passion narratives contain numerous minute details which could not have come from the same witness to the actual event. No primitive text from one witness could have been possible. A composition from many witnesses compiled by the author of the Gospel was indeed a necessity, since none of the evangelists witnessed the whole of what he reported. There must have been two different witnesses, for instance, in the garden, and at the trial before Pilate, since no Jew would have entered the pagan court willingly. Thus there was no unique account of the passion by any one witness. There were many different accounts of various witnesses concerning the events from Gethsemane to the resurrection apparitions.

As has been previously noted, almost all scholars agree that the most primitive text of the four Gospels is that of Mark. Was this Gospel the result of a grouping of several traditions? These same scholars also agree that there are two sources to which Mark referred. They disagree, however, on the details of these sources. V. Taylor,* for instance, proposes that Mark possessed an account of the passion which was simple, yet contained all of the essential elements of the passion. He hypothesizes that Mark would have completed his account with a certain amount of details obtained from Peter. Taylor bases this hypothesis on the fact that there is a heavy influence of Aramaic in certain passages. In addition, there are passages which are rather severe regarding Peter. Such severity toward the apostle Peter would have been unthinkable in the primitive Christian community unless it had its origin in the witness of Peter himself. Coupled with this is the fact that tradition has always associated Mark

---

* *The Gospel According to St. Mark* (London: Heinemann, 1953), 658.

with the apostle Peter. Taylor has a source "A," which was a basic document of the passion, written in correct Greek; and source "B," which is a series of additions of a different literary tradition, coming from Petrine sources. (Source "B": Ch. 14:3–9; 22–25; 32–42; 47–52; 54; and 65–72; Ch. 15:2; 6–14; 25; 27; 31–33; 38; 40–41; 47. The rest of the passion narration is from Source "A." This exemplifies at least one theory of modern scholars.

The second question, posed earlier, is just as difficult to answer. It concerns whether or not there is a special literary form for the passion account in each of the Gospels. There are many opinions on this subject, and we shall attempt to provide only a few.

Some scholars, among them M. Dibelius, have claimed that there is only one basic central fact in the passion narration, namely, that Jesus was crucified and died in Jerusalem. The details surrounding this central event were caused by various motives on the part of different Christian communities. Some of these motives are apologetical (with their scriptural arguments); others are homiletic, that is, designed for Christian preaching which had to consider the scandal of Christ's death. This theory overlooks the fact that in reality the preaching preceded the writing of the Gospels.

Other authors have claimed that the literary genre of the passion is similar to that of the acts of the martyrs since in these acts there are many details which were reminiscent of the passion account. Although it may be true to say that the passion was a prototype of the acts of the martyrs, there are details in the passion account which are not included in the acts of the martyrs.

Still others, Bultmann, for example, claim that the passion account is the development of the preaching of the good news by the primitive Christian community. Some hold that the text can be explained as a function of the liturgy of the Christian community. The Last Supper was the very center of the liturgical celebration, and the rest of the account was developed in connection with a more developed liturgy.

All of these theories can be understood only after we have examined the factors which influenced the formation of the Gospels themselves.

Factors in the Development of the Passion Narratives

The logical presumption here is that many things occurred between the triumphal entry of Jesus into Jerusalem and his crucifixion. However, only a few of these events are in fact preserved for us in the passion narratives of the Gospels. It is, therefore, logical to suppose that this was done for a specific reason in the final canonical Gospels. A choice was evidently made among the many details and eyewitness accounts of this central event in the life of Jesus. Yet the question remains, exactly why were these events chosen and not others?

The first observation which can be made about the early Christians and their eyewitness accounts of the events of the human existence of Jesus concerns their faith. They had no intention of "reporting" events *exactly* as they occurred, nor did they intend to achieve historical accuracy in every detail, as does a modern historian. Their objective was neither journalism nor history *as such*. They tell us of these events—which did in fact occur. Their accounts would otherwise have no meaning—in light of their faith. In other words, the Gospels are the witness of faith of the Christian community. It was not simply "the passion," but it was always "the passion of the Savior." This passion was the act of the God-man accomplishing the salvation of man. Thus when they spoke of the events surrounding the passion, they wanted to show how these events played a role in relation to their faith and how they accomplished the will of God (cf. the many citations from the Old Testament). The early Christians had to clarify and justify these terrible and scandalous events in light of their faith.

There must have been other primitive and simple confessions of faith even before the appearance of our canonical Gospels. We see this clearly in I Cor 15:3–7:

> For I delivered to you as of first importance what I also received, that Christ died for our sins in accordance with the scriptures, that he was buried, that he was raised on the third day in accordance with the scriptures, and that he appeared to Cephas, then to the twelve. Then he appeared to more than five hundred brethren at one time, most of whom are still alive, though some have fallen asleep. Then he appeared to James, then to all the apostles.

The repetitive nature of this confession shows that it was simple. It was the essential point of the Christian faith and was the witness of faith to these events by the disciples of Jesus. Christ died for the forgiveness of sins (its redemptive quality), and this death can be understood only in light of the resurrection, as God's witness and approval of the redemptive death of Jesus. The community tried to understand the terrible events of the passion in light of the resurrection of Jesus. This is why—as we shall see more clearly in our commentary—the texts of Second Isaiah concerning the suffering servant of Yahweh were so important in the passion narratives of the Gospels.

Scholars have also given four other motives, or preoccupations, which determined the choice of various events surrounding the Gospels for inclusion in the passion narratives. These factors are of a dogmatic, apologetical, exhortatory, and liturgical nature. We shall cover each of them briefly.

1. The Dogmatic Factor. This particular factor was perhaps the most important of all. In recounting the passion, it was the passion of the Savior of men who effected our salvation by his passion and resurrection. It was the resurrection alone which gave meaning to the passion and death of Jesus. Thus the *dogma*, or namely, that Jesus was the Son of God who died and rose, who suffered for and thereby saved men. This fact cannot be seen with the human eye. It can be seen only with the eye of faith. However, it was preached by the Christian community as a fact, as a *dogma* of the Christian religion. In this way only, the Chris-

tian could see who it was who died and rose.

2. The Apologetic Factor. The passion narratives, and therefore the passion itself, were used as an argument against the Christians. It was argued that Christ died an ignominious death like every other man. Moreover, his death was a scandal and a disgrace, since crucifixion was the lowest form of death that existed at the time. It was reserved for slaves and the worst criminals. Among Jews, the normal form of putting a man to death was by stoning. In the case of Christ, his enemies wanted to utterly crush him and all for which he stood.

By showing a publicly crucified Christ, all of the people could see what a terrible failure Christ was. They could see him totally and completely defeated. The fact that Christ died on the cross was used, for the Jews, as the supreme argument against the Christian religion. If he were the Son of God, how could God allow his Son to undergo such a shameful and ignominious death? The cross was the greatest scandal imaginable for ancient peoples. (There are sketches from first century Rome which depict a man with the head of an ass being crucified.) The Jews expected a glorious, conquering Messiah, and the Greeks expected an intelligent philosopher. To them, the greatest scandal was that the Christians claimed that a crucified criminal was the Savior of men.

3. The Exhortatory Factor. This factor was a natural tendency since many early Christians were already being persecuted for their faith. It was only natural to present the sufferings of Jesus as the exemplar for the sufferings and martyrdom of his disciples. The situation of Christ before his judges, and his condemnation to death, were all themes common to Christ and to Christians.

Those who preached the Christian message had to be prepared for suffering and death; they had their model in the person of Jesus. We can also see evidence of this motive in the beatitudes, partiularly Mt 5:10–11, which was formulated at the very beginning of Christ's public ministry. It was included in the Sermon to show Christians the redemptive value of suffering and persecution. In the passion account, the suffering Jesus is presented to Christians as a model to follow when they, themselves, are confronted with persecution for the Word. It must be Jesus alone in whom they put their faith and confidence during such times of trouble. Other writings of the New Testament develop very forcefully the theme that suffering for the Word is a most excellent way of being united to Christ.

4. The Liturgical Factor. The question of whether the liturgy of the community had any influence on the composition of the passion narratives has been raised by scholars in recent times. Some maintain that this was the central core of the narratives and that everything else revolved around this theme. As we shall see, however, there are few indications of this in our canonical Gospels.

Let us now investigate these factors more precisely in the passion narratives themselves.

The Dogmatic Factor. It is evident that this factor was primordial in the passion narratives. It was not simply the passion of an ordinary man. It was the passion of the Savior of men —a fact of faith, not of historical evidence. The facts of the crucifixion and death of Jesus formed an essential part of the Christian message and preaching. This theme was continuously present in the Acts, particularly in the discourses of Peter (Acts 3:11–26), Paul (13:15–41) and Stephen (7:2–3). All of these accounts stress the resurrection of Jesus after his death on the cross. Paul stresses this message more than once: "For I decided to know nothing among you except Jesus Christ and him crucified" (1 Cor 2:2). And again: "O foolish Galatians! Who has bewitched you, before whose eyes Jesus Christ was publicly portrayed as crucified?" (Gal 3:1.) The accounts of the crucifixion clearly show that these early Christians were not satisfied merely with the statement that Jesus was crucified; they went into minute detail concerning his death. They attempted to show the human aspects of the passion as well as the divine.

The human elements of the passion of Jesus were his sufferings and his innocence. From a human point of view crucifixion was one of the most painful of deaths; it was slow and excruciating. Death came to Jesus in a comparatively short time (as the result of the previous torture which he had endured). The evangelists describe the tortures and beatings of Jesus without great detail. The great violence was not emphasized. (Mark speaks of this in some detail, but Luke and John speak less of it.) The loneliness and solitude of Jesus are mentioned, but they are not stressed. Mark does relate the loneliness of Jesus on the cross, but John has Christ predicting the following: "The hour is coming, indeed it has come, when you will be scattered, every man to his home, and will leave me alone; yet I am not alone, for the Father is with me" (16:32). The Gospel of Luke does not depict Christ alone, for one of the robbers, crucified with him, becomes his disciple. In addition, Luke records the witness of the centurion after Jesus' death (Lk 23:47).

The divine factors concerning the death of Jesus are also brought out by the evangelists and, indeed, become the predominant ones in the passion accounts. Such were the titles which were applied to Jesus. For example, Mk 15:32 calls Jesus "The Messiah"; Mk 14:21 and 41, "The Son of Man"; Mk 14:61, "The Son of the Blessed One"; Mk 15:39, "The Son of God"; Mk 15:9 and 12, "The King of the Jews." When applied to Jesus, these titles have a transcendent meaning in the Gospels.

In the Gospel of John, the title most frequently used to designate Jesus is "Lord." The sacred kingship of Christ is emphasized throughout John's Gospel. Jesus is hailed as king during his triumphal entry into Jerusalem (12:13); Jesus proclaims himself a king before Pilate, although not of this world (18:33–37); on the cross itself, we have the title of king written in the three known languages of the time (universality): Hebrew, Latin and Greek. Thus, for John, Jesus on the cross becomes King both of the Jews and of all men.

The divine character of Jesus is also stressed by the fact that he foretells the passion events which are to occur. This is a trait attributed to Jesus throughout the Gospels. Jesus is never surprised at what happens to him. His passion was no accident of malice or fate; it was the will of God for the salvation of men, to which Christ freely assented. Christ's freedom throughout the passion is accentuated by all of the evangelists. Jesus goes to Jerusalem to suffer in spite of the objections of his disciples (Lk 13:31–34). The anointing at Bethany (Mt 26:6–13; Mk 14:3–9; Jn 12:1–8) was a clear foreshowing of his death, which he announces in Mk 14:49. The soldiers do not approach to take Jesus until he wants them to; and Jesus dies with the words which express his freedom, "All is accomplished" (Jn 19:30).

Christ is conscious of all of these events, knowingly and freely accepting them, desiring that they take place (Lk 18:31–34).This Jesus who suffered and died is the same one who rose from the dead, the Messiah and Son of God. The connection between the two is always kept by the evangelists.

The Apologetical Factor. As we have mentioned earlier, one of the foremost preoccupations of the early Christians was a defense against the attack of the Jews and pagans on the crucifixion of Jesus. For unbelievers, it was folly and stupidity, and an answer had to be given to these very serious allegations. The Christians tried to explain that what happened in the passion was prefigured and willed in the Old Testament, and that this influenced the choice of events of the passion itself, recorded for us in the canonicalGospels. These passages had a messianic meaning and were used to disprove the objections of the Jews. For instance, the appropriation of the clothes of a crucified man by the soldiers was a common occurrence, because a crucified man had no rights. The fact that the soldiers cast lots for the clothes is not an extraordinary happening. This was historically true during the crucifixion of Christ; however, that is not why it was noted in the passion accounts of the Gospels. This was reported because there was a messianic scriptural text from the Old Testament that stated: "They divided my garments among them, and for my raiment they cast lots" (Ps 22:18). This text served as an indication that Jesus was the Messiah. This very same observation might be made of the passage concerning the payment made to Judas by the priests and its subsequent return. This is narrated not to show the villainy of Judas but because there was a text from Zechariah (11:12), which mentions the payment of thirty pieces of silver as the "price of him who was priced."

Hence, certain episodes of the passion were chosen for narration because they resembled certain messianic texts of the Old Testament which the Jews could recognize; they showed the Messiah as a suffering Messiah. The evangelists took full advantage of these texts as an apologetical factor against the accusations of the pagans and Jews. This becomes more evident in the number of scriptural citations in the Gospel of Matthew, which was written specifically for the Jews. This was the product of the meditation of the Christian community concerning the Old Testament in light of the events of the passion itself.

There was also the important apologetic for the cowardly actions of the apostles during the time of the passion. Peter denied Jesus, and the others fled the master at his time of need. The only ones who were faithful to him were the women who had followed him on his journeys. The disciples immediately fled to Galilee to be safe from the government officials and Jews. Peter remained in Jerusalem, but he also denied Christ, not just once, but many times.

The Gospels make no effort to hide or attenuate this betrayal by the disciples. As a matter of fact, they bring out this aspect boldly and openly. In the course of time, however, we can clearly see an attempt by the community (and, consequently, by the evangelists) to mitigate this guilt. One can understand this tendency on the part of the community, since at the time of the composition of the Gospels the apostles had become their foundation stone and leaders; and it is humanly difficult to criticize one's leaders. In Mk 14:51–52, we find the story of the young man, present at the passion, who, being pursued by the police, fled naked after leaving behind the sheet which covered him. In Jn

18:1, the captors let the disciples of Jesus go free and thus in some way mitigate the guilt of the disciples. Indeed, it is Jesus who asks the captors to free his disciples. It was Jesus himself who predicted his abandonment by the disciples (Mt 26:31–35; Mk 14:27–31; Jn 16:32–33). Is this abandonment foreseen by Jesus, or does Jesus will it? Jesus emphasized that he must first suffer, be betrayed, die and rise again before they could be worthy witnesses to him.

Another example of this mitigation is the way in which the denial of Peter is treated in the various Gospels. The Gospel of Mark (derived from Petrine sources) is very harsh on Christ's betrayal by Peter. The later traditions (e.g., Luke) are not so harsh on Peter; they simply emphasize the fact of the betrayal itself. The power of the risen Lord served to show the weakness of the disciples. This weakness becomes a form of trust and confidence in Christ who can overcome all, including death.

The fact is that of all the disciples and followers of Jesus, only the women remained faithful to him until the very end. Mark lists their names but Luke mentions none by name. John adds that the mother of Jesus was there beside the beloved disciple. Thus some were faithful, and the infidelity is less and less emphasized by the evangelists—particularly in John, the last of the written Gospels.

We also have the case of the disciples who were asleep in the garden while Christ was in agony. Mark and Matthew both depict Christ rebuking them for not being able to pray for such a short time. Luke (22:45) provides an excuse for the disciples; they were asleep as the result "of sorrow."

The conclusion is quite clear: the primitive Christian community attempted to provide mitigating causes for the disciples' action because of their loyalty to their leadership. Nonetheless, they could not overlook it altogether because of their fidelity to the truth. It should also be clear that we have here a proof that these events actually did happen. Otherwise, the community would have refused even to record them, since they tended to show the imperfections of their leaders.

The apologetic motive was also present in the attempt by the evangelists to assign guilt to those who were responsible for the death of Christ, both to the Romans and to the Jews. The encounter of the primitive Christian community with official Judaism and Roman authority was influential in assigning this guilt. When opposition from the official Jews increased, the role of the Jews in the death of Christ was emphasized more; when this hostility increased from the Romans, their guilt was emphasized.

The canonical Gospels were written at a time when increasingly hostile relations existed between the early Church and Jews, whereas Roman authorities tended to regard Christianity as an offshoot of Judaism. The written Gospels, therefore, assign more guilt to Jews than to the Romans.

It is also clear that the early Christians were not particularly anxious to enter into conflict with civil authority. This explains why, in the narration of the passion, there is a tendency to excuse the Roman authority. Matthew depicts Pilate washing his hands of the whole affair, whereas he has the Jews call down guilt upon themselves and their children. Indeed, in John, Pilate is threatened by the Jews: "If you release this man, you are not Caesar's friend" (Jn 19:12), with the result that Pilate hands Jesus over to them. Luke (23:25) has the same thing. The blame is shifted from the Romans to the Jews in the apocryphal Gospel of Peter where it is Herod who pronounces the condemnation of Jesus. This same tendency can be seen in the episode concerning Barabbas, whom Pilate wishes to be condemned so that Jesus can be released. Pilate knows Jesus is innocent. It is the Jews, out of hatred, who demand the release of Barabbas and the condemnation of Jesus. The trial and beatings of Jesus tend to show a form of collective guilt. In this case, both Romans and Jews are implicated, and neither escapes censure by the evangelists. In Matthew, the whole Sanhedrin strikes Jesus, and in Luke Jesus is struck by all the men who are guarding him.

Thus there are some discrepancies in the Gospels concerning the proximate guilt of Jews and Romans. The events of the

passion are undoubtedly influenced by what was happening to
the Christian community between the years 40 and 80 A.D., yet,
there is a definite general respect for the truth. There is also the
bare fact of Christian antisemitism, which was awakened at this
time and had some influence on the narration of these events.
This poses the serious problem of trying to separate, very care-
fully, the clear teaching of Jesus (clearly not antisemitic) from
some passages in the Gospels which were influenced by a form
of antisemitism of the primitive Christian community. It is clear
from a study of the whole situation that the guilt for the death
of Christ must be shared both by some leaders of the Jewish
community, at one particular historical moment, and by some
Roman authorities in Jerusalem, at another particular historical
moment.

The Exhortatory Factor. As we have said previously, this
factor tended to show the relationship between Jesus and the
Christian community. The passion is a prototype of the passion
of Christians who were to follow Jesus in the early Church. Since
the disciple lives in imitation of Jesus, even in his death, he
continues the very death of Jesus. We see this in Acts 9:1–9,
where Paul encounters Christ on the road to Damascus: "I am
Jesus of Nazareth, whom you persecute." To do one thing to the
one is in reality also to do it to Jesus. This manner of imitation
of the passion is given clearly to us in the narration of the death
of Stephen, the first Christian martyr (Acts 6:9–8:3). We have all
the same ingredients: the trial and witness before the Sanhedrin
and the testimony of perjurers. The words of Stephen are those
of Christ on the cross, and death comes to him with a vision of
the Son of Man (cf. also 1 Peter 2:20–23; 3:17–18).

Many events of the passion were taken and applied to the
acts of the Christian martyrs. For instance, the betrayal of Jesus
by Peter is a sort of prototype for the betrayal of the Christian,
of faith in the face of adversity and death. Jesus heroically bore
witness to the truth even before the danger of death, but Peter
was a coward who fled from this witness. Jesus is then the model

for the Christian to follow in his own suffering and death before adversity. The whole witness of the apostles and of the Church is based on the confession of Jesus for Peter.

Another element of exhortatory nature given to us in the Gospels is that of Christ's sorrow in the garden. The soul of Jesus was sad, even unto death. So Christ is here once again a model for Christians who will also be sorrowful before the fact of death and persecution. The Spirit is willing but the flesh is weak. But, in spite of the sorrow, Christ accepts the sufferings of others.

A last example is present in the discourse of the Last Supper in Luke and John. Luke has a short discourse made up of several sayings of Jesus, probably pronounced under different circumstances but which now shed light on the events before the disciples: "I am in your midst as one who serves" (Lk 22:27). What this complete service was to entail would soon be revealed to the disciples (this saying in Matthew and Mark is located in the earlier part of the public life of Jesus: Mt 20:26–28; Mk 10:42–45). Luke places this saying in the discourse of the Last Supper. It illuminates the whole life and work of Jesus, and it indicates to the disciples how they are to act and serve.

The fact of the matter is that the Gospels were written rather late. They were written after much persecution and even after the death of some of the disciples. Therefore, it was quite natural that these events would influence their narration of these same Gospels. They attempted, thereby, to show the continuity between Master and the disciples who were persecuted and died for his name.

The Liturgical Factor. It is clear from a cursory examination of the Gospels that the Last Supper has certainly a liturgical flavor, particularly the words of the Eucharist. They were all pronounced at all the primitive liturgies, East and West. They are recorded for us in each of the Gospels, almost in the very same way.

The differences which are present, as we shall see, are caused by the different liturgical traditions present in the primitive Christian community. Thus in Mt 26:26 and Mk 14:22 the words are: "This is my body." In Lk 22:19 the words pronounced over the bread are: "This is my body, which will be given for you."* Presupposed in all of this, is the fact that this body of Jesus is *given* for the disciples in a sacrificial and loving way. This giving is expressed by Luke and by Paul. However, it is only understood in Matthew and Mark. Concerning the actual narration of the passion of Jesus (the third, sixth, ninth hour) we have no reason to believe that this corresponded to any liturgical motive.

What we do know is that the gospel was always read at the liturgical assembly. For instance, St. Hippolytus tells us that the Paschal liturgy consisted of a reading of the Gospel, baptism, and the Eucharist. But it seems rather clear that in the actual composition of the Gospels, it was only the Last Supper which was influenced by the liturgy of the ancient Christian community.

In conclusion, we may say that the Gospels are not really historical documents. They are testimonies to the faith of the early Christians who were influenced by the preaching of the Church. However, the apostles added their own personal touches. The preaching of the Church was, in its own turn, influenced by the above-mentioned motives. The events of the passion are narrated by men of faith. It is in this spirit that they pass it on to those who read their accounts. This influenced also the choice of events which the evangelist would report and the interpretation which he would give those events.

The next question to be posed is how the different episodes of the passion came to be grouped together. Were they recounted independently or as a total whole? Were they grouped according to a certain theme which the evangelists wished to stress? This was true of the first part of the Gospels, where Christ preached and healed. These events were assembled together by the evangelists without necessarily guaranteeing their exact

---

* Here we follow the Jerusalem Bible translation, not the RSV.

chronology. The main differences between the first and second parts of the Gospels is that the former were spread over a great time, whereas the passion was much shorter. It was, therefore, more constricting for the evangelists. This guarantees almost the exact historical succession of the events of the passion itself.

These accounts could have been given by different people, for example, Peter and the women who were at the cross and at the empty tomb. They could have been collected and put together by the evangelists. The accounts were put together with added scriptural references, which were the result of the meditation on these events by the early Christians. They were repeated by word of mouth and later put down in writing. The four accounts which have survived were the most important.

2

The Conspiracy Against Jesus

The first events of the passion given to us in the Gospels are those of the anointing at Bethany, the council of the chief priests against Jesus, and the betrayal by Judas.

The Treatment of the Passion in the Four Gospels

Mark. The introduction is very brief, and to the point, as is often the case with Mark. "It was now two days before the Passover and the feast of the unleavened bread. And the chief priests and the scribes were seeking how to arrest him by stealth, and kill him; for they said, 'Not during the feast, lest there be a tumult of the people'" (14:1–2). Mark gives us the date (Passover), those who are responsible for the conspiracy (high priests and scribes), their purpose (to kill Jesus), and the circumstances (the fear of a riot during the feastday). It is clear that this account of Mark is very simple and undeveloped. It is probably very primitive and authentic, very close to the original events. His theological meditation on these events (particularly if we compare Mark's account with John's) is almost nonexistent, itself a sign of its primitive nature.

Matthew. Matthew follows the same pattern as Mark but includes further details: "When Jesus had finished all these sayings, he said to his disciples, 'You know that after two days the Passover is coming, and the Son of Man will be delivered up to be crucified.' Then the chief priests and the elders of the people gathered in the palace of the high priest, who was called Caiaphas, and took counsel together in order to arrest Jesus by stealth and kill him. But they said, 'Not during the feast, lest there be a tumult among the people' " (26:1–5). He mentions that it is two days before the Passover, but he does not mention the feast of Azymes as does Mark. Nor does Matthew mention the scribes; he mentions the "elders of the people." This was a more juridical term than "scribes," for it designated members of the Sanhedrin, to which not all the scribes belonged. The emphasis was on the official leaders of Judaism: the ones responsible for the conspiracy to kill Jesus.

It is clear that Matthew must have used the account of Mark, which he developed and elaborated, with details of his own preoccupation. Matthew is fond of making reference to Old Testament texts that are fulfilled by Christ's passion and death. Thus we have a parallel in Deut 32:45: "And when Moses had finished speaking all these words to all Israel, he said to them. . . ." Is the similarity intentional? Would, then, Jesus be the new Moses? Indeed in the same text of Deuteronomy, Moses is commanded to go up to Mt. Nebo and there to die. These words are pronounced both by Jesus and Moses at the end of their lives or at the beginning of the end.

The statement of Jesus in verse 2 has both a theological and a biblical significance. Matthew is always anxious to emphasize the foreknowledge and acceptance by Jesus of the events of the passion. Jesus is portrayed as fully conscious of what is about to happen despite all the human machinations. Finally, Matthew adds the information that it was the Sanhedrin which was responsible for the conspiracy—a historical note added to the text of Mark in order to clarify the matter.

Luke. The text of Luke is similar to the texts of the above two evangelists, even though there are some minor differences. "Now the feast of Unleavened Bread drew near, which is called the Passover. And the chief priests and the scribes were seeking how to put him to death; for they feared the people" (22:1–2). The date in Luke is more vague than in Matthew and Mark. He also explains that the feast of Azymes is called the Passover, probably for the benefit of his non-Jewish audience. In general, the account of Luke is similar to that of the other two Synoptics, but he abbreviates his source, omitting many concrete details.

John. The text of the Gospel of John has its own context but still remains similar to that of the Synoptics:

> The chief priests and the Pharisees gathered the council, and said, "What are we to do? For this man performs many signs. If we let him go on thus, everyone will believe in him, and the Romans will come and destroy both our holy place and our nation." But one of them, Caiaphas, who was high priest that year, said to them, "You know nothing at all; you do not understand that it is expedient for you that one man should die for the people, and that the whole nation should not perish." He did not say this of his own accord, but being high priest that year he prophesied that Jesus should die for the nation, and not for the nation only, but to gather into one the children of God who are scattered abroad (II: 47–52).

The text is to be found immediately after the raising of Lazarus from the dead and before the triumphal entry of Jesus into Jerusalem (12:12–15). John mentions the fact that it was the high priests and the Pharisees who were responsible for the death plan for Jesus, which is not mentioned in the Synoptics. Thus we have the same event in John and the Synoptics, but it is thoroughly reworked from a different perspective in John.

The Anointing at Bethany

This event is narrated in each of the four Gospels. There is only one difference: in Luke (7:36–50) the event is not narrated in the context of the passion.

Mark.

And while he was at Bethany in the house of Simon the leper, as he sat at table, a woman came with an alabaster jar of ointment of pure nard, very costly, and she broke the jar and poured it over his head. But there were some who said to themselves indignantly, "Why was the ointment thus wasted? For this ointment might have been sold for more than three hundred denarii, and given to the poor." And they reproached her. But Jesus said, "Let her alone; why do you trouble her? She has done a beautiful thing to me. For you always have the poor with you, and whenever you will, you can do good to them; but you will not always have me. She has done what she could; she has anointed my body beforehand for burying. And truly, I say to you, wherever the gospel is preached in the whole world, what she has done will be told in memory of her" (14:3–9).

In Mark, the anointing takes place at Bethany in the home of Simon, the leper, while seated at table. A woman enters, bringing an alabaster jar of ointment of pure nard. Mark tells us that the ointment is costly. The woman breaks the jar and pours the contents on the head of Jesus. There are some (not named) who are indignant, since the cost of the expensive ointment could have been used for another good work. The woman is reproached for this, and Jesus comes to her defense by saying that the poor are always with the disciples, but not Jesus himself.

Matthew.

Now when Jesus was at Bethany in the house of Simon the leper, a woman came up to him with an alabaster jar of very expensive ointment, and she poured it on his head, as he sat at table. But when the disciples saw it, they were indignant, saying, "Why this waste? For this ointment might have been sold for a large sum, and given to the poor." But Jesus, aware of this, said to them, "Why do you trouble the woman? For she has done a beautiful thing to me. For you always have the poor with you, but you will not always have me. In pouring this ointment on my body she has done it to prepare me for burial. Truly I say to you, wherever this gospel is preached in the whole world, what she has done will be told in memory of her" (26:6–13).

The place where the event occurred was precisely the same place mentioned by Mark, but the fact that the ointment was of pure nard, or that the woman broke the jar, is not mentioned. "The disciples" were indignant, a more precise description than the "some" referred to in the Gospel of Mark. The same reason for the indignation is given, and Jesus defends by saying that it was done for his burial.

Luke.

One of the Pharisees asked him to eat with him, and he went into the Pharisee's house, and sat at table. And behold, a woman of the city, who was a sinner, when she learned that he was sitting at table in the Pharisee's house, brought an alabaster flask of ointment, and standing behind him at his feet, weeping, she began to wet his feet with her tears, and wiped them with the hair of her head, and kissed his feet, and anointed them with the ointment. Now when the Pharisee who had invited him saw it, he said to himself, "If this man were a prophet, he would have known who and what sort of woman this is who is touching him, for she is a sinner." And Jesus answering said to him, "Simon, I have something to say to you." And he answered, "What is it, Teacher?" "A certain creditor had two debtors; one owed five hundred denarii, and the other fifty. When they could not pay, he forgave them both. Now which of them will love him more?" Simon answered, "The one, I suppose, to whom he forgave more." And he said to him, "You have judged rightly." Then turning toward the woman he said to Simon, "Do you see this woman? I entered your house, you gave me no water for my feet, but she has wet my feet with her tears and wiped them with her hair. You gave me no kiss, but from the time I came in she has not ceased to kiss my feet. You did not anoint my head with oil, but she has anointed my feet with ointment. Therefore I tell you, her sins, which are many, are forgiven, for she loved much; but he who is forgiven little, loves little." And he said to her, "Your sins are forgiven." Then those who were at table with him began to say among themselves, "Who is this, who even forgives sins?" And he said to the woman, "Your faith has saved you; go in peace" (7:36–50).

The event takes place while Jesus is at the home of a Pharisee named Simon. The other basic events are the same as those related in Mark and Matthew. The event is situated during the first part of the public life of Jesus, probably in Capharnaum. The woman is described as a sinner, and Luke stresses her conversion. She pours the ointment on the feet of Jesus, instead of on his head, and then wipes his feet with her hair. She kisses his feet. All of this emphasizes the sorrow and penitence of the woman, to whom the divine forgiveness responds by forgiving her sins. The further development is also different from that of the other Synoptics. Simon continues, asking himself how Jesus can forgive sins, and Jesus then offers the parable of the creditors. Since the objective of Luke is different from that of the other two Synoptics, all references to the death and burial of Jesus are entirely eliminated.

John.

Six days before the Passover, Jesus came to Bethany, where Lazarus was, whom Jesus had raised from the dead. There they made him a supper; Martha served, and Lazarus was one of those at table with him. Mary took a pound of costly ointment of pure nard and anointed the feet of Jesus and wiped his feet with her hair; and the house was filled with the fragrance of the ointment. But Judas Iscariot, one of his disciples (he who was to betray him), said, "Why was this ointment not sold for three hundred denarii and given to the poor?" This he said, not that he cared for the poor but because he was a thief, and as he had the money box he used to take what was put into it. Jesus said, "Let her alone, let her keep it for the day of my burial. The poor you always have with you, but you do not always have me" (12:1–8).

As in Mark and Matthew, the event takes place in Bethany; however, the event takes place at the home of Lazarus and not at Simon's. The framework is in the context of a meal, at table, and the woman is positively named as being Mary, the sister of Martha and Lazarus. The ointment (genuine nard) is taken and poured on the feet of Jesus, with Mary wiping his feet with her hair. John adds something which was omitted by the other Gospels, namely, that "the whole house was filled with the fragrance of the ointment." John identifies Judas as the one who complains about the expense of the ointment, but he also specifies that it was not the result of his solicitude for the poor but because he was a thief.

We can conclude by saying that Luke is independent of Mark in his basic treatment of the event, that Matthew is quite close to Mark, and that John combines details from both Matthew and Mark.

Taking all of these divergencies into account, we can now attempt to reconstruct the actual event as it occurred and discover the significance given to it by the evangelists.

It is clear that the event is described differently in each of the Gospels. Mark's account is vivid, full of concrete imagery and colorful details. There is not much theological development, but there is some development in the mention of the burial of Jesus. This seems to indicate that the primitive Christian community was very sensitive to the fact that the body of Jesus was anointed and perfumed after his death, in keeping with the custom of the time. Many of the other forms of burial were forbidden him because of the rapidity with which he had to be buried. Thus the anointing at Bethany was seen by the Christian community as a substitution for the anointing that he was to be denied after his death.

Luke, as we have seen, developed this event outside of the passion, indicating that the event was recounted in some Christian circles outside of the passion proper. Luke gives us his own coloring. For instance, he notes that the woman is a prostitute, the archetype of the sinner, who comes near to Jesus and touches him. He uses this archetype quite often to show the difference in spirit (e.g., the publican and the Pharisee in the temple). She shows her repentant love completely, and she is defended by Jesus himself. Thus the main theme here is love and conversion.

John's account follows closely that of Mark within a definite plan of exposition. The event occurs in the house of Lazarus. This is important since, for John, Lazarus is the archetype of human death. Christ has come into the world to bring life to man, and he sees that it is communicated to Lazarus in the midst of human death. The whole purpose of the existence of Christ is given to us in Lazarus; it is the reason for his own death. Indeed, the first answer which Jesus gives to Judas is that of his burial, for this is the whole reason for his coming on earth. It is Judas who asks the question, while it is Judas who will be primarily responsible for the betrayal of Jesus.

From this cursory examination it is clear that there were two basic traditions, that of Mark and that of Luke. The essential element is the same in both cases, namely, that a woman comes to the house of Simon in order to anoint Jesus and thereby show her respect and love for him. The rest was a theological reflection by the community as it narrated these essential details (the anointing in function of the death and burial of Jesus). This whole episode was placed in a Paschal context by the community. The tradition of Luke retained the essential parts of the story, but it applied them in a different context. The details of the two traditions (Mark and Luke) are too similar to suppose two different anointings. Mark's tradition probably is the most primitive, but that of Luke is more faithful to the original event since it was not artificially situated within a Paschal context.

The Betrayal by Judas

There is a variant in this narration in Mark as opposed to that in Matthew: "Then Judas Iscariot, who was one of the twelve, went to the chief priests in order to betray him to them. And when they heard it they were glad, and promised to give him money. And he sought an opportunity to give him up" (Mk 14:10–11). This small narration gives us the full information: the name of Judas, what Judas did, and the important fact that he was one of the twelve. This created a great scandal for the Christian community when one of those chosen by Jesus actually betrayed him. Judas was then the archetype of the unfaithful or traitorous disciple. He betrayed Jesus to the high priests, the traditional protagonists of Jesus throughout the Gospels. The word chosen by the evangelist, "to give him up" *(paradidomi)* is an allusion to Isaiah 53 with reference to the suffering servant of Yahweh who was delivered up for the sins of his people.

The account in Matthew is as follows: "Then one of the twelve, who was called Judas Iscariot, went to the chief priests and said, 'What will you give me if I deliver him to you?' And they paid him thirty pieces of silver. And from that moment he sought an opportunity to betray him" (26:14–16). Matthew provides a dialogue of the actual betrayal rather than giving the bare facts. He mentions the thirty pieces of silver because there is a scriptural passage from the Old Testament to this effect: "And they weighed out as my wages thirty shekels of silver" (Zech 11:12). Linking Jesus' mission to Old Testament Messianism was one of the central preoccupations of Matthew.

The theology of Luke's account is even more developed: "Then Satan entered into Judas called Iscariot, who was of the number of the twelve; he went away and conferred with the chief priests and leaders how he might betray him to them. And they were glad, and engaged to give him money. So he agreed, and sought an opportunity to betray him to them in absence of the multitude" (22:3–6). Thus it is the adversary Satan who is in control of the situation. He departed from Christ after the temptation in the desert (4:13) and now once again enters the picture. Thus Satan plays a part in the passion. Luke also mentions the fact that the chief priests were afraid of the people.

3

The Last Supper and the Agony in the Garden

After these introductory remarks, we enter into the beginning of the passion proper, the meal which Christ took with his disciples on the night before his death. The meaning of this meal cannot be exaggerated since in it Christ explains to the disciples the meaning of the terrible events which are about to unfold.

Preparation

We know from the text of Mark that the meal was to be a Paschal meal:

And on the first day of Unleavened Bread, when they sacrificed the passover lamb, his disciples said to him, "Where will you have us go and prepare for you to eat the passover?" And he sent two of his disciples, and said to them, "Go into the city, and a man carrying a jar of water will meet you; follow him, and wherever he enters, say to the householder, 'The Teacher says, Where is my guest room, where I am to eat the passover with my disciples?' And he will show you a large upper room furnished and ready; there prepare for us." And the disciples set out and went to the city, and found it as he had told them; and they prepared the passover (14:12–16).

28

Mark thus situates the Last Supper on the first day of the unleavened bread, the first day of Matzot (Azymes), the day on which the Passover was immolated. The Last Supper was also then a Paschal meal.

The Passover was a feast celebrated each year by the Jews. Its origins go to the book of Exodus, where it was a form of double feast: the Passover properly speaking and the feast of Azymes. It was customary to offer God the first fruits of the land and flocks. This was in the form of a thanksgiving. So too, during the first harvest in April, the farmers offered new bread made from the new wheat without leaven. Thus the Passover was the feast of the shepherds, and Azymes was that of the farmers. They were united in Jewish tradition with the passage of the Jews from Egypt (Ex 12). When these gifts were offered by the Jews, the feast also evoked the memory of their deliverance from the slavery of Egypt. Therefore, the feast was not purely an agrarian or pastoral feast (a form of fertility rite); it slowly became a purely Jewish feast celebrating the deliverance of Israel. During the time of Christ, it was celebrated on a Friday, the day before the great Sabbath. During the previous night, the lamb which was previously slain in the temple was consumed at a supper. A description of this rite can be found in Ex 12:1–24.

We find, however, incongruities in the various Gospels concerning the exact day of the feast and, consequently, of the Last Supper. We really cannot harmonize them. In Mk 14:12 we are told that Jesus ate the Last Supper on the Passover. Jesus would then have been arrested on the night of the Passover and died on the same day. Yet, according to John, the Passover on that year fell on a Sabbath, and thus Jesus died on the Sabbath. Mark explicitly says that this could not have happened without a disturbance among the people. Thus there is a fundamental difference in the Gospels concerning the time of the Last Supper and the death of Jesus.

Mark, Matthew, and Luke place the Last Supper on the first day of Azymes, the day on which the lamb was immolated in the temple. It would seem from these accounts that Jesus died toward the end of the same day. Christ then would have died on the Passover. In Mk 15:42, Mt 27:62, and Lk 23:54, we are told that Jesus died on the preparation day, the day before the Sabbath; therefore, the meal of the Last Supper would have taken place at the beginning of the preparation day (Thursday).

The account of John, however, speaks of the Last Supper as if it were not a Paschal meal. He explicitly states that it was "before the Passover," but he gives his account of this supper after saying in the preceding chapter that the Passover was six days away. Moreover, John states explicitly that Jesus died on the eve of the Passover, rather than on the Passover itself (as the Synoptics state). Jesus did die on the preparation day, for the Passover that year according to John fell on a Sabbath (Jn 19:31), and if the Passover fell on a Sabbath, the eve of the passion fell on a preparation day. Thus in John, the Last Supper occurred at the beginning of the day before the Passover. John would agree with the chronology of the Synoptics by placing the death of Jesus on Friday, but he would disagree on whether it was a Passover or not.

Recent studies have attempted to resolve this difficult problem. A study by A. Jaubert* claims that not everyone in first-century Palestine agreed on the date of the celebration of the Passover. This is clear from a study of the texts of Qumran. Indeed the community at Qumran did not accept the date set by the temple officials; they celebrated the feast earlier in the week (the fourth day). Thus they did not eat the immolated lamb, which had to be sacrificed in the temple, nor did they observe the calendar set up by the temple officials. Jaubert believes that Jesus and his disciples were among those who celebrated the feast earlier in the week as did the monks of Qumran. This meal would have been eaten on a Tuesday, therefore, without a Paschal lamb, but they would have considered this a Paschal meal. When John says that Jesus died on the eve of the Passover, he must be referring to the official calendar of the temple officials.

---

* *The Date of the Last Supper* (New York: Alba House, 1965).

The events of the passion would have taken place between Tuesday and Friday evening since, contends Jaubert, it would have been impossible for all of the events of the passion to take place in the span of one evening. It is difficult to believe, however, that Jesus had the same mentality as those at Qumran. Although he and his disciples had broken with official Judaism, it was not for the same reasons which were operative with the monks of Qumran. Moreover, if Jesus had followed this calendar, there could have been no Paschal lamb and the meal would not have had the sacrificial character which the Synoptics give to it.

It must be said that the problem of chronology is a fairly important one because it deals with the deep symbolism of the Paschal and Passover meal in reference to the death of Jesus. Unfortunately, no satisfactory answer can be given, since the different chronologies found in the Gospels cause insurmountable difficulties. For the Synoptics the Last Supper would have been a Paschal meal, whereas for John it was a meal of farewell to the disciples. This makes little difference. In reality, the meal which Christ celebrated was not that of the Jewish law; rather, it was the new Pasch, in which Jesus himself became the new lamb of the new law. It was this aspect of the meal which was so important to the primitive Christian community.

In any case, the Synoptics place this meal in a Paschal context. The very question of the disciples to Jesus emphasizes this point: "Where do you want us to go and prepare for you to eat the Paschal meal?" The meal had to be eaten in Jerusalem and nowhere else. It is also clear that Jesus had no house of his own where the disciples could go to prepare for the meal—a sign of Jesus' poverty. He borrows everything he must use—even the ass on which he rides triumphantly in Jerusalem. Matthew has the disciples emphasizing the will of Jesus: "Where do *you* want ...?" The response of Jesus, "My time is near," likewise stresses the role of Christ's will in the passion. Jesus knows everything which is about to befall him.

The meal itself is described in Matthew and Mark with a liturgical motive from the community. The words pronounced

over the bread and wine (Eucharist) were probably taken from
the liturgical-eucharistic celebration of the community rather
than directly from the literal words of Jesus. But the significance
of the event is the same in all accounts—the blessing of the bread
and the cup: this is my body (flesh), and this is my blood which
is poured out. The details are different in the various traditions.
Those of Mark and Matthew are from Palestine, whereas those
of Luke and Paul (1 Cor 11:23–25) are from Asian tradition.

The Bread. The gesture of giving and eating the bread is
emphasized in Luke and Paul. Luke stresses that the bread "is
given for you" (Paul simply says "for you"). One of the variant
readings of the Luke passage also reads: "which is broken for
you." The actual fact of the giving is part of the symbolism, and
nothing more had to be added by Mark and Matthew. "To give"
was a technical word for the crucifixion. In the churches of Luke
and Paul, the import of this symbolic action was emphasized by
the addition of the verbal expression "given for you." The
theology throughout is that the body of Jesus is given to men for
the redemption of men.

The Cup. The traditions here are also different. The giving
of the cup is intimately connected with the death of Jesus on the
cross. As such, it is the symbol of the blood of Jesus to be shed
for men in order that they may participate in the new alliance.
The whole rite is performed in relation to the cross and has no
meaning without the cross. It is the Last Supper which begins the
whole mystery and participates in it (cross and resurrection).
John gives no indication that this eucharistic rite was celebrated
at the Last Supper. He transferred this doctrine in his Gospel to
chapter 6 and the disclosure of the bread of life. There is, however, one allusion to the Eucharist in his account: "He who ate
my bread has lifted his heel against me" (13:18). The text is from
the LXX (Ps 41:10), which he changes. The Psalm reads: "He who
eats [*esthion*] bread with me."

John reads, literally: "He who *chews* [*trogon*] bread with me" (cf. Jn 6:54). The substitution is quite intentional along with placing "bread" in the singular *(ton arton)* since this verb was used directly in 6:54 to describe the Eucharist: "He who *eats* [*trogon*] my flesh and drinks my blood has eternal life." The verb *trogon* (chew) is used in both places and is thus an allusion to the Eucharist. Those who have eaten the flesh of Jesus now betray him—the great scandal of the early Christian community. Yet, since John does not give us the institution of the Eucharist itself during the Last Supper, this seems to indicate at least one tradition in the community which does not recount the institution of the Eucharist with the rest of the passion. This may have been because the early Christians surrounded the Eucharist with secrecy, fearing it would be misunderstood by the pagans.

The Announcement of the Betrayal

The last instance during the meal was the announcement by Christ that he was about to be betrayed by Judas. The Gospels of Mark and Matthew record this event *before* the institution of the Eucharist, whereas Luke places it after the Eucharist. It seems that Mark and Matthew wanted to exclude Judas from the Eucharist, whereas in Luke and John, Judas actually participated in the whole of the Last Supper. He even received the Eucharist. Actually, the latter is probably what really happened. Mark and Matthew excluded him from the meal because he was a betrayer:

> And when it was evening he came with the twelve. And as they were at table eating, Jesus said, "Truly, I say to you, one of you will betray me, one who is eating with me." They began to be sorrowful and to say to him one after the other, "Is it I?" He said to them, "It is one of the twelve, one who is dipping bread in the same dish with me. For the Son of Man goes as it is written of him, but woe to that man by whom the Son of Man is betrayed! It would have been better for that man if he had not been born" (Mk 14:17-21).

The fact that they were at table is repeated twice in order to emphasize the fact that the betrayer ate with Jesus, since the meal is regarded as a sign of fraternity. Those who ate together shared the same food and therefore, in a sense, shared the same life. The meal was a family affair and those who partook of it were considered to be brothers. Thus when Christ says that one of those who is eating with him is about to betray him, it is only to emphasize the enormity of the deed as a betrayal of friendship and brotherhood.

The whole scene is symbolic for the Christian community since each disciple is in constant danger of betraying Jesus. Each Christian who betrays Jesus is like Judas since Judas was the first to eat at the table of Jesus and then betray him. Each Christian, like Judas, has an intimate relationship with Jesus. Judas thus became the archetype of all Christians who would betray Jesus.

Luke adds a discourse composed of various sayings which were probably pronounced earlier, and in another place, since the other evangelists record them earlier (Mk 10:.42–45 10:42–45;Mt 20:25–28). These sayings mean that the disciples, like Jesus, are to serve rather than be served, just as Jesus does even to the point of death. These sayings illuminate the entire life and death of Jesus and reveal their meaning for the disciples. It is probably for this reason that Luke places these sayings here.

The Agony in the Garden

This setting is found in Mk 14:32–46 and in Lk 22:40–46. Thus: "They came to a country place which was called Gethsemane" (Mk 14:32). "They" are the disciples and Jesus. The situation is clarified in John (18:1), where we read that Jesus is arrested in a garden, his headquarters while he was in Jerusalem. The word "Gethsemane" is nothing more than the Greek transcription of the Aramaic word meaning "olive press." It was situated on the other side of the valley of the Cedron from the city of

Jerusalem just across from the temple. The reason for going there was to pray: "Sit here while I pray" (Mk 14:32). This is theologically important since prayer serves to prepare Jesus for the agony which he will experience during the next hours. Moreover, through the prayer in the garden, he fully and freely accepts all the events which will follow. The passion for Jesus was not a quirk of fate; it was the consciously planned will of Jesus.

Taking the disciples, Jesus instructs them: "And he took with him Peter and James and John, and began to be greatly distressed and troubled. And he said to them, 'My soul is very sorrowful, even to death; remain here and watch'" (Mk 14:33–34). This passage is similar to Gen 22:5, where Abraham spoke to his servants as he was about to take his son Isaac up to be sacrificed: "Stay here with the ass; I and the lad will go yonder and worship, and come again to you." The wording in Mark and Matthew is intentionally similar to that in Genesis.

Why were Peter, James, and John chosen to be more intimately associated with the prayer and agony of Jesus? They did have a special role to play during the public life of Jesus, and they are presented as constantly asking Jesus questions. It could be that these disciples played an important role in the establishment of the Church at Jerusalem and were thus considered special among the twelve and "pillars of the church" (Gal 2:9). They were the sole witnesses of the transfiguration and agony of Jesus in the garden.

The relationship between the transfiguration and the agony in the garden is emphasized because the same three disciples bore witness to the two events. This cannot be without some significance, since the transfiguration itself was a preparation for the Paschal mystery, and it is Jesus himself who says this (cf. Mk 9:9): "And they were coming down the mountain, he charged them to tell no one what they had seen until the Son of Man should have risen from the dead." Mark adds that the three disciples were asking themselves what the connection was or what this rising from the dead actually meant. This evokes curiosity, since good Jews knew what resurrection was. It was part of their teaching. What they could not understand was the resurrection of Jesus, who would actually die and rise again. How could Jesus die? A being from heaven cannot suffer or die. It was shown to them in the transfiguration itself that Jesus was a heavenly being. Jesus, one moment later, says that he is going to suffer, die, and rise again. This was indeed strange for the disciples. Yet Christ deliberately joined the two events since he was the suffering servant of Yahweh (cf. Mk 8:31): "He began to teach them that the Son of Man must suffer many things, and be rejected by the elders and the chief priests and the scribes, and be killed, and after three days rise again."

Once again, the disciples did not understand him; in fact, Peter reprimanded Jesus for saying this. They could not understand the meaning of a suffering Messiah. Thus we can appreciate the great confusion and consternation of the disciples throughout the narration of the passion, for this was a crisis of their faith. They honestly believed that Jesus was the Messiah, but they could not reconcile this belief with suffering and death, nor did the passion of Jesus fit into their concept of the Messiah. Jesus claimed to be from God; yet he suffered and died, and God did not come to his aid and save him. What the disciples expected and what they witnessed were diametrically opposed. The women were not so shaken in their faith because they adhered to him not by theory but by love. For this reason, they did not abandon him when they did not understand what was happening. There can be no understanding of the passion of Jesus without the resurrection of Jesus.

Mark stresses that the sorrow of Jesus in the garden was deep and abiding: "And he . . . began to be greatly troubled and distressed. . . ." The word "troubled" *(ekthambeisthai)* means to be profoundly agitated, a ripping and tearing state of anguish. The word "distressed" *(adaemonein)* indicates a strong state of upheaval and trouble. This state overcomes Jesus to the point of having "his soul troubled even to death." Jesus frequently speaks of his soul (Mk 8:36–37; Lk 12:19), and this expression can be found in the Old Testament as well. It means one's whole being and not the Greek idea of spiritual principle of man.

The whole being of Jesus is profoundly in sorrow (cf. Ps 42:6; Jonah 4:6). The sorrow of Jesus is so strong that only death can put an end to it. The reason for this sorrow is given to us in the prayer of Jesus: "And going a little farther, he fell on the ground and prayed that, if it were possible, the hour might pass from him" (Mk 14:35). Jesus, overcome by grief, goes on a little farther from the chosen three to pray. This is normal; throughout the Gospel Jesus prays alone (Mk 1:35–39; Lk 5:16). Even when Jesus teaches his disciples how to pray, he says, "when *you* pray." Jesus never says, "let us pray." His relationship to his Father is unique and different from that of the others; he goes off alone to pray.

Mark says that "Jesus fell to the ground." This is crude in that it expresses brutally the fact that Jesus experiences the feeling of complete defeat. Matthew is less harsh: "He fell on his face," which can be a normal position of prayer among orientals. Luke goes even further in trying to attentuate the feeling of Jesus by saying that Jesus kneels down to pray. Mark is the most vivid of the three in expressing this overwhelming feeling of Jesus.

Jesus prays that "this hour might pass from him." The "hour" of Jesus is a key term in the Gospels, indicating the successive stages of the plan of God. Jewish apocalyptic literature used this expression quite frequently to indicate the end of the world. This would be the signal for a new world from God and formed by God, putting to an end the present time. This is called "*the* day" or "*that* day," or "the day of the Lord" (cf. Dn 8:17; 19). This "hour" signifies the passage from the old to the new world. This hour coincides with the passion of Jesus. Jesus prays that the hour pass from him because it is a time of trial and of suffering. This was the specific difference between Jewish apocalypses and the passion of Jesus: in order for this hour to come, Jesus had to suffer and die.

A Comparison of Parallel Texts Concerning the Prayer of Jesus

Mark is the only evangelist to give us the Aramaic word for Father, *Abba*. "Abba, Father, all things are possible to thee; remove this cup from me, yet not what I will, but what thou wilt" (Mk 14:36). The word was commonly used by Christians to express their intimate relationship with God. We see this in the various letters of Paul (Rom 8:15; Gal 4:6). The word itself is difficult to translate, but it means Father, with emphasis on the tenderness and kindness of a father. It is much like the English word "daddy." Since it was difficult to translate, the early Christians simply kept it in its Aramaic original. A parallel exists between the prayer of Jesus and the prayer of Christians. Mark emphasizes the faith of Jesus: "all things are possible to thee" (cf. Gen 18:14).

Jesus asks that this "cup" pass from him. The theme of the "cup" is found throughout the New Testament, but with different nuances. One can have a cup of joy represented by its contents, wine; here it symbolizes the feast itself (Ps 16:5; 23:5; 115:4). The cup is also presented as a bitter one, containing a bitter drink (Ps 10:7; 75:9; Is 51:17-21; Jer 25:15-18; Ez 23:31-34). The aspect of bitterness is emphasized in the New Testament (cf. Mk 10:38). Drinking the cup represents something undesirable which involves suffering and pain. It is, however, presented as being necessary before sharing in glory. It is the first condition of entering the messianic banquet. Jesus in the midst of his pain asks the Father to release him from what is to come. The personal desire of Jesus is fully expressed, but his wish is completely subordinate to the will of the Father. Mark stresses the full obedience of Jesus before his passion and death. Jesus freely and fully accepts the divine will and all that goes with it, for only by doing the will of his Father can Jesus achieve the redemption of men.

Redemption, its accomplishment and reception, must be fully free. From this follow full confidence and trust in God, who can do all things. The drama in the garden is the lot of all Christians, and each in his turn is called on to respond to the will of God. It was not the suffering of Jesus which brought about the salvation of men but rather the obedience of Jesus to the will of his Father. The passion and death of Jesus in reality receive their efficacy from his obedience to the Father's will.

Jesus then finds the three disciples asleep: "Simon, are you asleep? Could you not watch one hour? Watch and pray that you may not enter into temptation: the spirit indeed is willing, but the flesh is weak" (Mk 14:37–38). Why did the disciples fall asleep? Perhaps because they were simply tired, "for their eyes were heavy" (Mk 14:40). Luke states that they were asleep because of sorrow. Here the theological meaning is that the disciples were asleep because they did not understand the importance of what was happening during that time. Their sleep is a sign of miscomprehension. Instead of being awake and watching these eschatological events—for only he who watches and prays will be prepared for their coming—those who "sleep" run the risk of not realizing that salvation is at hand. They may miss the supreme eschatological event. They enter into temptation with the result that, if they are not awake, they will someday realize that they have failed during their miscomprehension. "Wakefulness is the only way to overcome this great temptation. The action of those who are awake is prayer, but this is not an easy task since the flesh is weak and good will does not suffice.

The example of Christ is clear as he watches and prays during that fateful time and thus overcomes temptation. Mark notes that Christ goes back three times for prayer and prays for hours. The prayer of Jesus is persistent in the face of trial and temptation. When Jesus returns for the third time he says: "Sleep on now and take your rest. It is enough; the hour has come; the son of man is betrayed into the hands of sinners" (Mk 14:41). Jesus here—and throughout the Gospel—gives himself the title of Son of Man. It is a reference to Daniel 7, where the Son of Man is portrayed as a being of divine origin who comes to earth at the appointed time. It is therefore a messianic title. The hour is the beginning and consummation of the passion of Jesus when he is handed over to the sinners, who now seemingly have control of the whole situation. It is in this *hour* that Jesus finds himself completely alone without any worldly protection whatever. He refuses heavenly aid as well as human force (Peter's sword). In his abandonment to God's will, Jesus finds the complete freedom which has been prepared by his prayer to his Father. The disciples, who have misunderstood everything, now flee.

The whole scene in the garden is based on two separate sayings of Jesus, the prayer to his Father and the words to his disciples; and it seems that they are not very well combined. They seem to be from two different traditions or narrations of what happened on that fateful night. The first concerns Jesus himself, his prayer, temptation, the theme of the hour, the cup, and the consent of Jesus to the passion. The second group of sayings, or memories, concerns the disciples of Jesus and his exhortations to them. The most logical source is the apostles themselves, with emphasis on the parallel between the Christian and Christ's example in the garden. Thus the vigilance, the temptation, and the hour of the disciple are contained in this series of narratives.

Mark would have united them into one whole, but the literary attempt is quite evidently a failure; not much of an effort is made to harmonize the diverse elements into a unified whole. Jesus returns very abruptly from his prayer to the disciples, and, in Mk 14:41, says to the disciples, "sleep and take your rest." Mark must have recorded the traditions as he found them with little attempt to harmonize them. The accounts of Matthew and Luke correct this.

The text of Matthew reads: "Then Jesus went with them to a place called Gethsemane, and he said to his disciples, 'Sit here while I go yonder and pray'" (26:36–46). The stress is on the person of Jesus, who is accompanied by the disciples, whereas Mark had simply "they." As we have previously mentioned, Matthew substitutes the word *lupeisthai* ("I am sorrowful") for the very strong word *ekthambeisthai* ("I am greatly distressed") used by Mark. Instead of throwing himself on the ground because of his sorrow, the Matthean Jesus lies on the ground, almost in a liturgical fashion. In the prayer of Jesus, the Aramaic "Abba" disappears, and "if it be possible" is substituted for Mark's "all things are possible to thee!"

In general, there is little difference between the texts of Mark and Matthew. The only difference seems to be that Matthew completes or embellishes the account of Mark.

The account of Luke (22:40–46) is essentially an abridgment of Mark's text. His preoccupation is to limit Jesus' sense of defeat. The very human aspect of Jesus being crushed to the ground is omitted by Luke. Moreover, Jesus kneels to pray rather than lie down or be thrown to the ground by his sorrow. There are some points in the narration which are proper to Luke: he says that "there appeared to him an angel from heaven strengthening him." The figure of an angel here conveys the sense of God's aid and help in comforting Jesus in his suffering since God supports those who call upon him. Luke also adds that the sweat of Jesus dropped down as drops of blood upon the ground, an expression of great pain and suffering. Anguish is often accompanied by sweating. The disciples were asleep because of sorrow—here we have, perhaps, an attempt by the Christian community to attenuate the guilt of the disciples. In general, however, Luke's account is substantially like Mark's.

The Gospel of John does not even mention the agony in the garden. He situates the arrest of Jesus in the garden but mentions neither prayer nor exhortation. John simply states: "After saying these things, Jesus went forth with his disciples beyond the torrent of Cedron, where there was a garden into which he and his disciples entered" (18:1). The arrest follows immediately.

John places the anguish of Jesus in a context other than that of the garden. "When Jesus saw her weeping, and the Jews who came with her also weeping, he was deeply moved in spirit and troubled . . . " (Jn 11:33). The context is the death of his friend Lazarus. When Jesus arrived in Bethany, Lazarus had been dead for four days and the household was in the midst of mourning. The reaction of Jesus would seem to be a human reaction to the death of a dear friend. Yet this reaction of Jesus has a deeper meaning than that of a purely human character. Jesus is not weeping for his friend—this is absurd since he will raise him immediately—but rather for his own death. He sees the sorrow which human death brings to people, and he is troubled by this. The result of this sorrow is that he raises his friend Lazarus back to life, a symbol of his own death and resurrection.

Jesus is troubled by death—all death—including the death which even he will experience. "And Jesus answered them, 'The hour has come for the Son of Man to be glorified. . . . Now is my soul troubled. And what shall I say, Father, save me from this hour? No, for this purpose I have come to this hour' " (Jn 12:23–28). Once again Jesus is troubled by the thought of death.

The theme of the "hour" is here, as it was in the Synoptics (v. 23). Mark portrays the hour as that time in which Jesus is handed over to the hands of sinners. John's hour is the time of the glorification of Jesus. There is no opposition, since John gives us a more synthensized view of the situation. Then follows a small parable (v. 24) about dying and living. It is death which will give life, and this theme is used to shed light on the Paschal mystery of Jesus. The death of Jesus is a necessary precondition to his entering into the full glory of God. Without death there can be no life. This is true for Jesus, and consequently is all the more true for his disciples to whom Jesus says: "He who loves his life loses it, and he who hates his life in this world will keep it for eternal life. If any one serves me, he must follow me . . . if any one serves me, the Father will honor him" (Jn 12:25-26). In order to have life, the Christian must die with Jesus.

Jesus is troubled at the prospect of his own death, just as he was when confronted with the death of Lazarus in chapter 11. The reaction here is internal, and the reason for this anguish is that he finds himself faced by his own death. He then asks his Father to be released from this burden but is submissive to the Father's will—here John echoes the Synoptics. He wills the passion because this is why he was sent into the world. The glory of God will be manifest in the hour of Jesus through the events which are about to be acted out. "When Jesus had said these things, he was troubled in spirit, and said solemnly, 'Amen, Amen, I say to you, one of you will betray me' " (Jn 13:21). This occurs during the Last Supper and is very close to the passage of Mark in which we read that the hour is the time when Jesus is betrayed into the hands of sinners.

4

The Trial of Jesus

After his arrest, Jesus was first taken before the Jewish authorities of the time. His trial was twofold, one by the Jews and the other by the Romans.

The Trial before the Jewish Officials

There is disagreement among the evangelists concerning the first stage of the trial before the Jewish officials. Mark and Matthew mention two meetings with the Jewish officials, one at night and the other in the morning. Luke mentions only one meeting, in the morning. John mentions only one, but it takes place at night. The Synoptics place the trial at the home of Caiaphas or at the official meeting place of the Sanhedrin. John claims that it takes place at the home of Annas.

Mark introduces the trial by stating that the men who arrested Jesus took him at night to the high priest, who would have been Caiaphas (14:53). Peter comes and follows at a distance, where he awaits outside in the courtyard for what is to happen to Jesus inside (v. 54): "Now the chief priests and the whole council sought testimony against Jesus to put him to death" (v. 55). Hence it was the Sanhedrin which sought to kill Jesus. The chief priests were those from whom the high priest was chosen.

They belonged to the official council. The Scribes were the official theologians and doctors of the nation. The elders were the influential members of the community because of their age and experience. This group united to do away with Jesus (we have seen their intention during the conspiracy). Hence, it was not a trial in the true sense of the word. It was a travesty of justice to give legal cover to their foreordained intentions. Moreover, it was not a legal meeting, since that body could not be convened at night.

The text of Matthew draws heavily from Mark. Matthew actually names Caiaphas and states that the others were assembled in his home. Mark continues: "Now the chief priests and the whole council sought testimony against Jesus to put him to death. But they found none. For many bore false witness against him and their witness did not agree" (Mk 14:55-56).

According to Jewish law, no man could be condemned for any crime without witnesses (at least two), who had to agree on what was said (Dan 13:1-64). Thus two such witnesses could not be found since they were either false or disagreeing. Theologically speaking, this former charge is a value judgment by the Christians, for one would have to be a believer to make this acknowledgment. The witnesses did not agree and consequently, according to Jewish law, the man could not be condemned. He had to be juridicially freed from the charges.

Matthew, however, unifies more than did Mark, and he thereby perfects Mark. Matthew states only that it *was* a question of false witnesses who were unable to come to a formal condemnation of exactly what was said or done. We are not told why the testimony was proved worthless or how the witnesses were lying.

The testimony of the witnesses is important in Mark's account: "And some stood up and bore false witness against him, saying, 'We heard him say; I will destroy this temple that is made with hands, and in three days I will build another, not made with hands.' Yet not even so did their testimony agree" (Mk 14:-58-59). The witnesses are presented as being false, as well as in

disagreement with each other. They stated that Jesus opposed
the temple of Herod to another not made by men.

The concept of a temple not made by hands was common
in Jewish apocalyptic literature. It was to be an eschatological
temple of messianic times in a new earth and a new world. On
that day, all the institutions of earth will be made new. The
temple of Jerusalem is the sign of the new and future temple to
be built by God (cf. Apoc 21:1–18). It is Jesus who will play an
essential role in relating and closing these two worlds in their
transition. Jesus will bring the present time to a close and begin
a new era, a new eon. Jesus will be the essential mediator in this
transformation that is soon to happen ("three days").

When this testimony is presented against Jesus, the clear
implication is that the person who announced an event of this
magnitude would himself be claiming to be the Messiah or the
one who would bring this apocalyptic event about. It is this
testimony and the silence of Jesus which will cause the high
priest to ask Jesus directly whether or not he is the Messiah.

This testimony has its root in the Gospels themselves and
is based on the cleansing of the temple of the money changers
by Jesus. This event is reported in the Synoptics after the entry
of Jesus into Jerusalem. Indeed, Matthew and Luke place it on
the same day, whereas Mark places it one day later. The Synoptics end their account of this event by saying: "And he taught,
and said to them, 'Is it not written, "My house shall be called
a house of prayer for all the nations?" But you have made it a
den of robbers' " (Mk 11:17).

John recounts the event in a different context, at the very
beginning of the public ministry of Jesus. Jesus is not only *the*
prophet (sensitive to the things of God and zealous for God's
house) but also is someone who has direct authority in this
matter. The messianic message is evident here: "And in those
days the merchant shall be no more in the house of the Lord"
(Zech 14:21). In this context John quotes directly from the LXX
translation of the Old Testament: "The zeal of thy house has
eaten me up" (Ps 69:10).

John deliberately changes the tense from the past to the future: "Zeal for thy house *will* consume me" (Jn 2:17). The sign which Jesus gives the Jews to authenticate the authority with which he does these things is the resurrection: " 'What sign do you give us for doing this?' Jesus answered them, 'Destroy this temple, and in three days I will raise it up.' The Jews then said, 'It has taken forty-six years to build this temple, and you will raise it up in three days?' But he spoke of the temple of his body" (Jn 2:18–21). The Greek word for "raise," *egeiro*, is the same word used in Scripture with regard to the resurrection of Jesus. The disciples did not understand the significance of this event until after the resurrection of Jesus. This whole section is an affirmation of the messianic role of Jesus made to the Jews of his day.

In parallel texts, Matthew relies on Mark and adds nothing to what Mark has already told us. We can now understand why the high priest asks Jesus directly whether he is the Messiah or not: "And the high priest stood up in the midst, and asked Jesus, 'Have you no answer to make? What is it that these men testify against you?' But he was silent and made no answer. And the high priest asked him, 'Are you the Christ, the Son of the Blessed?' And Jesus said, 'I am; and you will see the Son of Man sitting at the right hand of power, and coming with the clouds of heaven' " (Mk 14:60–62).

The high priest stood up as a sign of power in the assembly. Jesus gave no answer and simply permitted his accusors to give any testimony they wished. Perhaps this is an allusion to the suffering servant of Isaiah 53, who spoke no word against those who beat and insulted him. Next is the central question of whether Jesus is the Messiah. The "anointed one" or "Messiah" of God was anointed in view of a particular function here as king, priest, and prophet of the future kingdom. His coming would signal the beginning of the last or eschatological times. The "blessed one" is God himself. Being a good Jew, the high priest would never have pronounced the name of God. The reference is clearly in Dan 7:14 and two other passages of the Old Testament as well. For instance, in Ps 2:1 we read: "You are my son, this day have I begotten you." The tendency in Judaism was to identify the Messiah with a form of sonship with God, at least as a sign of close association, so that no one could arrogate the title to himself without blasphemy.

The passage from Matthew is somewhat different from that of Mark. The formula used here is: "I adjure you by the living God: tell us if you are the Christ, the Son of God" (Mt 26:63). These two titles—Christ and Son of God—were those given to Jesus by the early Christian community; thus they are full of meaning in Matthew. Luke has only "Christ."

The answer of Jesus is extremely important for the whole development of the New Testament.

In Mark, even the various Greek manuscripts are not in agreement. Some have: "You have said that I am." Yet the majority of the manuscripts simply have the affirmation of Jesus: "I am" *(ego eimi)*, which means "I am who you say I am." Matthew and Luke are more ambiguous. They have: "You have said so" (Matthew) and "if I tell you, you will not believe, and if I ask you, you will not answer" (Luke). These are ambiguous statements since they can be taken as follows: "It is you who is saying that I am." Yet this ambiguity is immediately cleared in the continuation of Jesus' answer, when there is evident an allusion to Daniel 7.

Daniel describes a heavenly being who comes down from God to earth with the power of heaven to establish a new kingdom. Jesus claims that the Jews will see the establishment of this reign or kingdom. The messianic implications of this title are quite evident. Jesus claims the heavenly power to establish the kingdom of God on earth. Yet Jesus does not use the titles "Son of God" or "Messiah" to describe himself. This was especially the case in the public life of Jesus, for he did not wish to confuse his role in the minds of the people who were mostly expecting a temporal Messiah. Only Peter gives this title to Jesus: "Simon Peter replied, 'You are the Christ, the Son of the living God.' And Jesus answered him, 'Blessed are you, Simon Bar-Jona! For flesh and blood has not revealed this to you, but my Father who is in heaven' " (Mt 16:16–17). It is clear that this knowledge comes to Peter only by the grace of God, for no human instrument could reveal this to him. We may therefore explain the ambiguity in Mt 26:64 and Lk 22:67 by saying that it is in keeping with Jesus' own unwillingness to use this title. By avoiding the use of such a title, Jesus avoids being caught up in the political aspirations of priests and people. In fact, immediately after the confession of Peter at Caesarea, Jesus speaks of the death on the cross —which is a prerequisite for the establishment of Christ's kingdom. He is the Messiah according to the will of God, not according to the will of man.

It is this question which the high priest asks of Jesus. Jesus answers that he is this Messiah, but the Sanhedrin understands the title in a political and social sense and not in the meaning given that title by Jesus. In Mark, Jesus answers clearly that he is the Messiah—as distinguished from the rest of his Gospel, which has Jesus keeping this a secret. At this decisive moment Jesus makes his intention clear, and he now speaks openly before the leaders of Judaism.

Jesus referred to himself as the "Son of Man" many times throughout the Gospels, and indeed it is the only title which he explicitly gives himself in the Gospels. The title obviously comes from the book of Daniel: "I saw in the night visions, and behold, with the clouds of heaven there came one like a Son of Man, and he came to the Ancient of Days and was presented before him. And to him was given dominion and glory and kingdom, that all peoples, nations and languages should serve him; his dominion is an everlasting dominion, which shall not pass away, and his kingdom one that shall not be destroyed" (7:13–14). Jesus uses this title in a double series in the Gospel.

The first series comprises the apocalyptic discourses of Mk 13:36, Mt 24:26, 30; Lk 17:22, 26; 21:27. The meaning here—as in our present text—is very clear, that is, he describes himself in the context of the Son of Man in Daniel. In the passage, this "Son of Man" is seated at the right hand of God (the euphemism of "power" is given). Jesus will share in the power of God, which has come down from heaven in the person of Jesus. The son of man is representative of the power in establishing God's kingdom on earth. It is in this sense that Jesus makes claim to his messianism, and it is this which the Sanhedrin understands.

The second series of texts is scattered in various places in the Gospels during the public life of Jesus: "For which is easier to say, 'Your sins are forgiven,' or to say, 'Rise and walk?' But that you know that the Son of Man has authority on earth to forgive sins . . ." (Mt 9:6). The scribes and others were scandalized that Jesus made claim to forgive sins as this was the prerogative of God alone. Jesus exercises his power in healing the sick man as a sign of his ability to forgive sin. This same intention can be found in Mk 2:28: "The Son of Man is Lord even of the Sabbath."

There is a third series where this title is used almost exclusively in regard to the death of Jesus. In Mt 20:18–19 we are told that the Son of Man will be delivered to the Gentiles, beaten, and crucified, and that on the third day he will rise again. So too, in Mk 10:45 and Mt 20:28, the Son of Man has come not to be served but to serve.

In itself, the expression "Son of Man" in oriental languages means simply a man of flesh and blood. Ezekiel refers to himself in this way in order to emphasize that he was only a man among others with nothing special about him: "Again the word of the Lord came to me: 'Son of man, behold, they of the house of Israel say . . .' " (12:26, 13:2).

In which sense did Jesus use this title? It is clear—as in our present text in the passion—that the reference is to the "Son of Man" in Daniel. In other places the title is used by Jesus precisely because it is so ambiguous. In Mt 9:6 the audience knew full well that Jesus was making claim to the title in the book of Daniel; for it was in virtue of his heavenly power that he could forgive sins even here on earth. But his listeners had to make this conclusion themselves since the title was ambiguous. Evidently Jesus uses the title in the messianic sense of Daniel.

Jesus is a being always united to God, and he is inseparably associated with the divine power in heaven and on earth. This power of God for salvation, however, will be realized fully only through the passion and resurrection of Jesus. The ambiguous use of the title during the public life is easily understandable. Jesus did not wish the people to come to false conclusions as to his salvific role. This title is preserved for us only in the Synoptics, the Acts of the Apostles and the Gospel of St. John. It did not survive in early Christianity since it was much too ambiguous. Very soon these Christians substituted the title "Son of God" for the title "Son of Man." The evolution of the former title, which depended in great part on the Hellenistic milieu in which the Church emerged, cannot be developed here.

As we have said, in the passion narrative Jesus is very clear about the meaning of the term "Son of Man." The words of Christ following his confession leave no room for doubt. He is not the political Messiah the Jews expected; he is the "Son of Man," seated at the right hand of the power of God. This declaration was directly responsible for Jesus' death. Jesus is *the witness* to God before those who hate him and will finally kill him. Nevertheless, Jesus gives his testimony courageously—a model for Christians to follow.

The reaction of the high priest is symbolic of the supposed blasphemy committed in his presence. The rage of the high priest is obvious. Jesus asserts a claim which could only seem scandalous to a good Jew. Before them stood a weak and simple man who made pretense to divine power.

Only Mark reports that they condemned Jesus. They probably did not condemn him, since it was illegal for the Sanhedrin to meet at night. Matthew and Luke correct this in their accounts. They found him guilty but could not pronounce condemnation. Moreover, a condemnation of death on the cross had to come from Pilate, who alone had the *jus gladii*. The sentence, however, had already been decided. Mark tells us: "Some began to spit on him, and to cover his face, and to strike him, saying to him, 'Prophesy!' And the guards received him with blows" (14:65). There are two kinds of insults here: the first was delivered by the Sanhedrin ("some"), the other by the police. Matthew does not distinguish between the two. Jesus presents himself as the Messiah and the guards mock him for this.

Mark includes a second trial, or consultation, to review the case of Jesus. "And as soon as it was morning, the chief priests, with the elders and scribes, and the whole council held a consultation" (15:1). The reason, as previously explained, was that all official business by the Sanhedrin had to be performed during the day. The purpose was to "deliver him to Pilate." Matthew mentions two trials, whereas Luke and John mention only one. The second trial recorded in Matthew and Mark is perhaps based on the fact that the beginning of chapter 15 in Mark originally belonged to another tradition; thus 15:1a could have simply been a resumé of the preceding events serving as an introduction to the trial before Pilate. Mark simply would have respected the source and included it as it was.

The Trial before Pilate

The Roman authority in Jerusalem was represented by Pontius Pilate. Flavius Josephus speaks of him in his *Jewish Antiquities*, Book 18, Ch. 3, no. 1–2; Ch. 4, no. 1–2 and in his *Jewish Wars*, Book 2, Ch. 9, no. 2–4. He portrays for us a man of immense cruelty and violence who continuously, during his ten-year stay (26–36 A.D.), provoked the Jews, whom he hated. It seems that Pilate was antisemitic; he probably followed the example of the Emperor, Tiberias Caesar. An example of his provocation was to mint money for Palestine which bore a graven image. Yet Josephus could have been prejudiced, and it seems that his judgment of Pilate was more severe than that of the evangelists. The Gospels portray Pilate as a Roman functionary doing a job and not wanting to risk any disfavor in Rome over an insignificant Galilaean.

Mark records the following dialogue: "And Pilate asked him, 'Are you the king of the Jews?' And he answered him, 'You have said so.' And the chief priests accused him of many things. And Pilate again asked, 'Have you no answer to make? See how many charges they bring against you.' But Jesus made no further answer, so that Pilate wondered" (15:2–5).

We have here a summary of the trial with the central question being asked by Pilate The chief priests presented Jesus to Pilate as a sort of troublemaker, possibly a conspirator against the power of Caesar, claiming to be the Savior (in a political sense) of Israel. They understood, or at least attempted to make Pilate believe, that the claim of Jesus was political, whereas they wanted to preserve law and order by denouncing such a troublemaker. Jesus' answer to Pilate's question is again ambiguous. Jesus remains silent to the many charges made against him, a characteristic attitude throughout the passion. Perhaps there is an intended allusion to the suffering servant of Isaiah 53, who was "mute as a lamb before the shearer."

The account of Luke is somewhat different. He develops the accusation of the Jews against Jesus in a political vein: "And they began to accuse him, saying, 'We found this man perverting our nation, and forbidding us to give tribute to Caesar, and saying that he himself is Christ a King . . .' But they were urgent, saying, 'he stirs up the people, teaching throughout all Judea, from Galilee even to this place'" (23:2, 5). Jesus is accused of being a political king and before this charge he is silent.

Mark includes the episode of Barabbas:

> Now at the feast he used to release for them one prisoner whom they asked. And among the rebels in prison, who had committed murder in the insurrection, there was a man called Barabbas. And the crowd came up and began to ask Pilate to do as he was wont to do for them. "Do you want me to release for you the King of the Jews?" For he perceived that it was out of envy that the chief priests had delivered him up. But the chief priests stirred up the crowd to have him release for them Barabbas instead" (Mk 15:6–11).

Although we have no official records of this practice, it was quite probable, since the Roman authority had almost unlimited power in his own jurisdiction. In addition, prisoners were considered to have no rights whatever. Barabbas (Bar-abba, "son of the father") was simply a murderer who was apprehended during "the insurrection." We do not know to which insurrection it refers.

The "crowd" calls for the release of Barabbas, who is portrayed as a murderer and a man of violence. Jesus, however, throughout the Gospel, is always portrayed as a nonviolent person who refuses all recourse to violence. The crowd chooses violence instead of Jesus and, in this sense, is opposed to the crowd which welcomed Jesus into Jerusalem. This latter crowd was essentially nonviolent as they saluted and accepted Jesus riding on the back of an ass, the symbol of peace and nonviolence.

The title which Pilate uses to identify Jesus recurs throughout the Gospel. He sees that the Jews want to condemn Jesus not for wrongdoing but because of divisive religious issues, which Pilate holds in contempt. Pilate then has to release Barabbas since he already has placed Jesus on the same level with Barabbas, who had been found guilty of murder. Otherwise, Pilate would not be seeking to "free" Jesus. Pilate is maneuvered into handing Jesus over to be crucified. It is noteworthy that not even Pilate ever condemns Jesus. He *delivered* him to the Jews and throughout the passion "delivered" was a technical word for the injustice suffered by Jesus.

Before Pilate handed Jesus over, he had him scourged:

And the soldiers led him away inside the palace (that is, the praetorium); and they called together the whole battalion. And they clothed him in a purple cloak, and plaiting a crown of thorns they put it on him. And they began to salute him, "Hail, King of the Jews!" And they struck his head with a reed, and spat upon him, and they knelt down in homage to him. And when they had mocked him, they stripped him of the purple cloak, and put his own clothes on him. And they led him out to crucify him (Mk 15:16–20).

This was a Roman scourging and as such it was limitless. Indeed many victims were known to have died from the shock alone. It is ironic to note that Pilate considered this flagellation as an act of mercy, for he thought the Jews might relent at the sight of a beaten man (Luke and John). Moreover, since crucifixion would normally take a long time, a good flagellation would help speed up the process of death, thereby decreasing the overall sufferings of the victim. Thus to Pilate the scourging was an act of compassion.

Matthew 27:15 has the following: "Now at the feast the governor was accustomed to release for the crowd any one prisoner whom they wanted." This sentence stresses the good will of Pilate. He continues: "And they had then a notorious prisoner, called Barabbas. So when they had gathered, Pilate said to them, 'Whom do you want me to release for you, Barabbas or Jesus who is called Christ?' For he knew that it was out of envy that they had delivered him up." "They" refers to the Jews in general. Matthew wanted to place the principal blame for the death of Jesus on the Jews in general, not just the chief priests and scribes. The incident of Pilate's wife (v. 19) is not recorded in any other part of the New Testament. There seems to be no reason why this episode is included; it does not follow logically anything in the text. It is a secondary detail of little importance and perhaps is left here by Matthew because he found it in some secondary tradition concerning the passion.

Matthew (27:24–26) adds the episode of the washing of the hands by Pilate and the guilt of the crowd who shout: "His blood be on us and on our children!"

In Luke's account, the narration is much shorter than that of Mark or Matthew with a significant difference. Pilate (23:18–19) appears more anxious to release Jesus than he does in the other two Synoptics. Moreover, Luke claims that it was not Pilate who took the initiative to release Barabbas, but the crowd. Pilate declares Jesus to be innocent in two places: "I find no crime in this man" (23:4). "Pilate then called together the chief priests and the rulers and the people, and said to them, 'You brought me this man as one who was perverting the people; and after examining him before you, behold, I did not find this man guilty of any of your charges against him' " (23:13–15). Pilate is opposed by the crowd. He is intimidated by it, and he punishes Jesus in order to placate it. It is evident that Luke wants to put the major blame on the Jews and not on the Roman authority. Pilate merely approves the decision of the crowd, seeking to exonerate himself of the decision. The reason for this could be that Luke was writing for Christians converted from paganism, and he consequently wanted to attenuate the guilt of the Roman authority.

The Gospel of John is much more elaborate in this particular area of the passion. John attaches great importance to the trial before Pilate and includes a very well-developed dialogue between Jesus and Pilate. Both before the Jews and the Roman authority, Jesus defends his teaching concerning his kingship. He does not remain silent as he did in the Synoptic accounts. Although both the Synoptics and John focus the issue on Jesus' claim to be a king, John attaches a different significance to the term:

> Pilate entered the praetorium again and called Jesus, and said to him, "Are you the King of the Jews?" Jesus answered, "Do you say this of your own accord, or did others say it to you about me?" Pilate answered, "Am I a Jew? Your own nation and chief priests have handed you over to me; what have you done?" Jesus answered, "My kingship is not of this world; if my kingship were of this world, my servants would fight that I might not be handed over to the Jews; but my kingship is not from the world." Pilate said to him, "So you are a king?" Jesus answered, "You say that I am a king. For this I was born, and for this I came into the world, to bear witness to the truth. Everyone who is of the truth hears my voice." Pilate said to him, "What is truth?" (Jn 18:33–38.)

In the Synoptics Jesus was accused of making claims to royalty, but in a political sense (cf. Mk 15:9, 12), and before this charge Jesus is silent. In John, Jesus answers Pilate directly, acknowledging himself as a king, but not a human power who must defend himself by force. Indeed, if his were an earthly kingdom, the only way to defend it would be by violent means. Peter did strike Malchus, but he was promptly rebuked by Jesus, and the damage was repaired (18:11).

Violence is clearly against the intention of Jesus. The answer baffles Pilate, since there could be no possible case against Jesus by Caesar, if this were true. Jesus would threaten no one, including Caesar himself. Pilate cannot understand what kind of kingship Jesus is talking about. The kingdom of Jesus is without boundaries and without violence or force; it is made up of all those who have seen and accepted the truth. Yet, for John, truth is God himself, which proclaims God himself; the only way to enter this kingdom is by accepting the Word of God, which is truth. Not all can enter this kingdom, for some do not or cannot recognize the truth of God. Only those who hear, understand, and are obedient to God's word can enter this kingdom. There are those who simply refuse the light (cf. Jn 1:9–13). Pilate responds with the answer of a skeptic for whom there is no real truth, only political expeediency to maintain law and order.

From this point forward in John's account, Jesus is silent and no longer speaks to Pilate, who does not and cannot understand what Jesus is talking about. Jesus only brings the word to those who can understand or who want to understand; to the rest, confusion, misunderstanding, and silence. John reveals to us the meaning of Christ's kingship.

The dialogue ends. After unsuccessfully trying to release Jesus, Pilate attempts to soften the Jews by having Jesus scourged.

> Then Pilate took Jesus and scourged him. And the soldiers plaited a crown of thorns, and put it on his head, and arrayed him in a purple robe; they came up to him saying, "Hail, King of the Jews!" and they struck him with their hands. Pilate went out again, and said to them, "Behold I am bringing him out to you, that you may know that I find no crime in him." So Jesus came out wearing the crown of thorns and the purple robe. Pilate said to them, "Here is the man" (19:1–5).

Since the questioning during the trial centered around the kingship of Jesus, the mocking by the soldiers took a form of torture
which included the crown of thorns and the purple cloak. Prisoners were men without rights. They were at the perfect mercy of
the police. This whole incident had profound meaning for John
and the early Christians. They saw the royal enthronement of
Jesus entering his glory in the process of becoming king. It is
completed when Jesus ascends the cross, and it is this royalty of
Jesus which John continuously underlines throughout the passion narratives. The soldiers are the first to celebrate the exaltation and glorification of Jesus.

Pilate is presented by John as trying to free Jesus, whom he
knows to be innocent. Even the beating of Jesus was intended
to soften the hearts of the Jews. The crowd, however, is violent
and murderous and calls for his crucifixion. Jesus had claimed
to be a king, and this was a crime. Yet the true reason now comes
to the fore: "The Jews answered him, 'We have a law, and by that
law he ought to die, because he has made himself the Son of
God' " (19:7).

Formerly, in the trial, the chief priests accused him of political evil; now they proceed to the properly religious plane and
claim that Jesus has made a divine pretention, not just a messianic one. This frightens Pilate, who once again attempts a
dialogue with Jesus. As we have seen, Jesus remains silent before
a man who cannot understand his words (v. 9). Pilate attempts
to threaten Jesus (v. 10), but Jesus reverses the threat by remind-
ing Pilate whence his power came (God) and to whom he must
answer for any wrongdoing.

Pilate desperately wants to release Jesus, but the crowd
threatens Pilate with his job (v. 12). The morality of his action
does not bother him as much as the danger to his position. He
can afford to be objective as long as he is not directly involved,
but when he does become involved, his job is threatened, and his
objectivity simply ceases.

Then he handed Jesus over to them to be crucified (v. 16).
Pilate will be denounced as a traitor to Rome, and in order to
save face he continues the formality of a trial:

When Pilate heard these words, he brought Jesus out and sat down on the judgment seat at a place called The Pavement, and in Hebrew, *Gabbatha.* Now it was the day of the preparation of the Passover; it was about the sixth hour. He said to the Jews, "Here is your King!" They cried out, "Away with him, away with him, crucify him!" Pilate said to them, "Shall I crucify your King?" The chief priests answered, "We have no king but Caesar" (19:13–15).

The chronology in John does not agree with that of Mark or Matthew. Mark and Matthew claim that Jesus was crucified at the third hour, whereas John says that judgment was being passed at the sixth hour. It is evident that John places it at noon since it was the exact hour of the Parasceve, or preparation day, for the Passover when the lambs in the temple began to be slaughtered. Since John sees Jesus as the new Paschal lamb, he makes the slaughter of the lambs coincide with that of the new lamb of God. The new Paschal meal and sacrifice have begun.

The theme of the royalty of Jesus once again is found here. John has Pilate hand Jesus over for crucifixion, when the chief priests finally admit that they have no other king except Caesar. Here, we have the beginning of the new Paschal feast and the end of Israel, since the true Israel throughout her history had recognized only Yahweh as its king. This statement of the priests marks the end of the old economy. Even the inscription imposed by Pilate brings out the royalty of Jesus:

Pilate also wrote a title and put it on the cross; it read, "Jesus of Nazareth, the King of the Jews." Many of the Jews read this title, for the place where Jesus was crucified was near the city; and it was written in Hebrew, in Latin, and in Greek. The chief priests of the Jews then said to Pilate, "Do not write, 'The King of the Jews,' but 'this man said, I am King of the Jews.' " Pilate answered, "What I have written, I have written" (19:19–22).

The new kingdom of Jesus, as well as his kingship, is consummated on the cross. The inscription on a cross was common among the Romans. It indicated to passersby the nature of the crime committed. John attaches great importance to it since the three languages were those of the entire known world of that time. John wishes to show the universality of the salvation of Jesus to all peoples and nations. The inscription is a sign of the accomplishment of the royalty and kingship of Jesus on the cross for all men. Jesus becomes king on the cross, which is his throne in a universal kingdom. The writing of Pilate is thus an unconscious prophecy of what was indeed happening. This also occurred with Caiaphas when he prophesied that one man has to die for the whole people. Pilate cannot retract what he has written, for he has unconsciously written only the truth.

It is an interesting question to ask the source of the supplementary information of the passion which John gives us. For instance, the dialogue between Jesus and Pilate is not found in the Synoptics. John could have used another tradition, whereas this was unavailable to the Synoptics. Second, John could have been more or less an eyewitness to these events; he tells us that the "other disciple" was known to the high priest and succeeded in having Peter introduced into the courtyard. Third, John takes great freedom with his material for the purpose of showing the profound religious meaning of the events of the life of Jesus. John is one who communicates a truth rather than a historical event. His main concern is symbolism, and he directs his material toward that end. These events cannot be understood in their material value but only in their symbolic meaning. They reflect divine realities.

5

The Crucifixion and
Death of Jesus

The soldiers requisitioned a passer-by to help Jesus with the cross. Since Palestine was under military occupation, it was a fact that soldiers simply took the first able-bodied man they could find to do the work. As a result of the flagellation, Jesus could not carry his own cross. The Gospel gives us the man's name: Simon of Cyrene. "And they compelled a passer-by, Simon of Cyrene, who was coming in from the country, the father of Alexander and Rufus, to carry his cross. And they brought him to the place called Golgotha (which means the place of a skull). And they offered him wine mixed with myrrh; but he did not take it" (Mk 15:21–23).

According to some, Simon was a pagan, but there is no proof for this. His sons have Latin or Greek names, which was a common practice among the Jews of the diaspora. Paul probably makes a reference to them in Rom 16:13. This part of Mark's Gospel was probably a memory kept by the family of Rufus and Alexander.

The Fourth Gospel would seem to contradict this account of Mark: "So they took Jesus, and he went out, bearing his own cross, to the place which is called the place of the skull, which is called in Hebrew Golgotha" (Jn 19:17). These two documents could easily be reconciled by saying that Jesus started to carry his own cross but, because he had been so weakened by the flagellation, could not continue and thus had to be helped by Simon.

We must, however, look at the theological perspective of each Gospel. As we have seen, Mark is simply recording a memory of the family of Rufus and Alexander. He does not attach much theological importance to it. Both Luke and Matthew fail to mention Rufus and Alexander; they had little meaning for them. Being faithful to Mark, however, they mention Simon.

Matthew and Luke seem to give it a theological significance. For Luke, Simon does what every Christian must finally do. Indeed, Lk 23:26 uses the same formula found in Lk 9:23: "If anyone wishes to follow me, let him deny himself and take up his cross daily and follow me." The Christian must follow in the steps of Jesus, sharing the cross of Jesus just as Simon did. Luke understands the symbolism in the event. He drops some of the details and places more emphasis on the theology than does Mark. Moreover, Luke stresses the fact that Simon carried the cross *behind*, or after, Jesus, and in 9:23 Luke says that the Christian must follow Jesus.

John's theology is such that it is only Jesus who carries the cross, only he who bears the whole weight of redemption.

The Crucifixion

Jesus was taken outside the walls of the city to be crucified since Jewish law forbade any violent death in the city of Jerusalem itself (Mk 15:20). They made him remain close enough to teach others a lesson in law and order. "And they crucified him, and divided his garments among them, casting lots for them, to decide what each should take. And it was the third hour, when they crucified him" (Mk 15:24-25). Crucifixion was the ancient form of deterrent. Outside the wall there was a large rock about fifteen feet high. According to Origen, the skull of Adam was supposed to have been found there, a story which, of course, has no historical value whatsoever.

Then we read: "And they offered him wine mingled with myrrh; but he did not take it" (Mk 15:23). As an act of mercy common among Jews (cf. Pr 31:6), a form of anaesthetic was given to condemmed criminals. Myrrh, mixed with a little wine, created great drunkenness. The condemned man would thus enter his suffering without experiencing it. Jesus refused, not because he wanted to suffer but because he wanted to enter into the event consciously.

The Gospels describe the crucifixion very simply with no attempt to underline the terrible torture of a Roman cross, along with its humiliation. Mark puts it simply: "And they crucified him" (15:24). The crucifix itself could take different forms: it could be a simple pillar or in the shape of a crossbar or in the shape of an "X." The prisoners could either be tied or nailed to the wood. The Fourth Gospel refers to the wounds of Jesus (Jn 20:25, 27). From this, we can conclude that Jesus was nailed to the cross. The humiliation was also a factor—one which would end only with death. Since no vital organs were injured, the victim would die slowly and painfully, usually from exposure and lack of food and drink. The era was a cruel one, and the crucifixion was a sign of the inhumanity of the times.

The Garments. "They divided his garments among them, casting lots for them" (Mk 15:24b). The property of a condemned man belonged to those who crucified him or to the public authorities. These soldiers simply divided what Jesus had on his person. This offers John a perfect opportunity to quote from Ps 21:18: "They parted my garments among them, and for my clothing they cast lots."

The Time. Mark divides the event into three periods. He says that Jesus was crucified at the third hour (9:00 A.M.), that darkness spread over the earth at the sixth hour (12:00 noon), and that Jesus died at the ninth hour (3:00 P.M.). The other Synoptics and John mention only the sixth and ninth hour. We have seen already the symbolic nature of the time element for St. John.

There were other men crucified with Jesus: "And with him they crucified two robbers, one on his right and one on his left" (Mt 15:27). Jesus' crucifixion is presented as only one of several that were performed that day. John agrees with Mark (19:18), but he does not mention that they were robbers. Later, Mark tells us that they too ridiculed Jesus (v. 32b). There is no theological development of this episode in Mark. Once again, here Jesus is in the midst of the poorest of humanity. Luke has the episode of the "good thief," which is another extension of the solicitude of Jesus for even the dregs of humanity. We have here a small summary of the story of redemption: sinfulness of man, belief in Christ who saves, and salvation. Indeed, Jesus is in union with the sufferings of even the poorest of men.

Humiliation by the bystanders was a standard part of a crucifixion: "And those who passed by blasphemed him, wagging their heads, and saying, 'Aha! You who would destroy the temple and build it in three days, save yourself, and come down from the cross.' So also the chief priests mocked him to one another with the scribes, saying 'He saved others; he cannot save himself. Let the Christ, the King of Israel, come down from the cross, that we may see and believe.' Those who were crucified with him also reviled him" (Mk 15:29–32). The word Mark uses is blaspheme *(eblasphaimon)*. The people mocked him by calling on him to make use of his special powers to save himself: "And those who passed by blasphemed him, wagging their heads, and saying, 'You who would destroy the temple and build it in three days, save yourself! If you are the Son of God, come down from the cross' " (Mt 27:39). "And the people stood by, watching; but the rulers scoffed at him, saying, 'He saved others; let him save himself, if he is the Christ of God, his chosen one!' The soldiers also mocked him, coming up and offering him vinegar and saying, 'If you are the King of the Jews, save yourself' " (Lk 23:35).

All of these people call on Jesus to prove himself by using his power, if he had any. The formulation of these insults stems from the trial before the Sanhedrin, where Jesus was accused by false witnesses of having said that he would destroy the temple and in three days would build it up again. Logically, if Jesus could do anything, he would certainly do it now in order to save his life. Humanly speaking, the whole passion of Jesus was a sign of his weakness and defeat just like any other man who is condemned to suffer and die. To the Jews, this was a clear sign that he was not a man of God, for God had abandoned him at this most crucial hour.

The second insult came from the high priests. They take their text from the Old Testament book of Wisdom, which gives a description of the just Jew who is the object of antipathy for those Jews who have betrayed Yahweh:

> *For they reasoned unsoundly,*
> *saying to themselves,*
> *"Short and sorrowful is our life,*
> *and there is no remedy when*
> *a man comes to his end,*
> *and no one has been known*
> *to return from Hades.*
> *Because we were born by mere chance,*
> *and hereafter we shall be as though*
> *we had never been;*
> *because the breath in our nostrils is smoke,*
> *and reason is a spark kindled by*
> *the beating of our hearts.*
> *When it is extinguished, the body*
> *will turn to ashes,*
> *and the spirit will dissolve like empty air.*
> *Our name will be forgotten in time,*
> *and no one will remember our works;*
> *our life will pass away like*
> *the traces of a cloud,*
> *and be scattered like mist*
> *that is chased by the rays of the sun*
> *and overcome by its heat.*

For our allotted time is the passing
        of a shadow,
and there is no return from our death,
because it is sealed up and no one
        turns back.

"Come, therefore, let us enjoy
        the good things that exist,
and make use of the creation
        to the full as in youth.
Let us take our fill of costly wine
        and perfumes,
and let no flower of spring pass by us.
Let us crown ourselves with rosebuds
        before they wither.
Let none of us fail to share in
        our revelry,
everywhere let us leave signs of
        enjoyment,
because this is our portion, and this
        our lot.
Let us oppress the righteous poor man;
let us not spare the widow
nor regard the gray hairs of
        the aged.
But let our might be our law of
        right,
for what is weak proves itself
        to be useless.

"Let us lie in wait for the righteous man,
because he is inconvenient to us
        and opposes our actions;
he reproaches us for sins against
        the law,
and accuses us of sins against
        our training.

He professes to have knowledge of
  God,
and calls himself a child of
  the Lord.
He became to us a reproof of our thoughts;
the very sight of him is a burden
  to us,
because his manner of life is unlike
  that of others,
and his ways are strange.
We are considered by him as
  something base,
and he avoids our ways as
  unclean;
he calls the last end of
  the righteous happy,
and boasts that God is his father.
Let us see if his words are true,
and let us test what will happen at
  the end of his life;
for if the righteous man is God's son,
  he will help him,
and will deliver him from the hand
  of his adversaries.
Let us test him with insult and torture,
that we may find out how gentle
  he is,
and make trial of his forbearance.
Let us condemn him to a shameful death,
for, according to what he says,
  he will be protected."

The text describes the attitude of a group of men who did not remain true to Yahweh and who find in the just man an insupportable rebuke to their lives. They put him to a test to see whether God will aid him. The attitudes of the chief priests seem to be the same as this group described in Wisdom. Here God does not intervene on behalf of Jesus.

The third insult is that only if they see Jesus come down for the cross will they believe: seeing is believing. Thomas said this, and Jesus rebuked him for it (Jn 20:29). So too the chief priests refuse to believe until they see for themselves.

The story of the good thief is introduced here by Luke who is the only evangelist to record it for us. The other thief railed and insulted Jesus (23:39). One of the thieves has a change of heart and defends Jesus (v. 40–42). Then follows his request to be with Jesus in his kingdom. The answer of Jesus is simple: "Truly, I say to you, today you will be with me in Paradise" (Lk 23:43). It is an astounding response since the word "Paradise" is never used by Jesus in the Gospels.

Jesus also promises the good thief that he will be in paradise *today*, thus a consciousness of something beyond death—salvation. This salvation can be attained only through death. The good thief is assured of entrance into this paradise, today, after his death. Yet this "today" is not the today of the present time, it is the today which will be, a today which begins with death and continues. In saying this, Jesus is conscious not only of saving himself but also of his power to grant this entrance to others. The good thief is an example of the violent man who snatches the kingdom of God. His violence is not due to his crimes but to the simplicity of his faith.

The only difficulty with this whole passage is that the other Synoptics portray both thieves insulting Jesus. Although the good thief could have changed his attitude, there seems to be no agreement in the two accounts. Moreover, the doctrinal implications of the episode are remarkable. Luke could have received this episode from a more primitive source than the other two Synoptic Gospels. This is shown by the fact that the passage uses the rather archaic and unusual word "Paradise." The essence of the story remains that a poor man seeks mercy even in a desperate hour; he sees what others (e.g., the chief priests) do not and cannot see. By his simple faith, God gives him salvation. This episode sums up the whole theology of man's redemption by Jesus.

The Death of Jesus on the Cross

"And when the sixth hour had come, there was darkness over the whole world until the ninth hour" (Mk 15:33). Some, Lagrange, for instance, hold that this darkness was caused by some natural phenomenon, such as a heavy wind or storm. This is to miss the whole object of the evangelist's intent in recounting this event. Mark attempts to show that the whole of creation is somehow touched by this event. This is a literary device, making the natural phenomena of the scene the author is describing correspond to the very meaning of the events. It is a form of "atmosphere creation" in which the author fits the event. This is similar to the scene in the book of Amos 8:9–10: " 'And on that day,' says the Lord God, 'I will make the sun go down at noon, and darken the earth in broad daylight. I will turn your feasts into mourning, and all your songs into lamentation; I will bring sackcloth upon all loins, and baldness on every head; I will make it like the mourning for an only son, and the end of it like a bitter day.' "

Many images are evoked to describe the sadness of the end of Israel; for example, mourning, dirge, and sackcloth. The sun, being a symbol of joy, is darkened and this gives a feeling of anguish. The mourning for an only son is the worst form of loss. This is a literary device to portray the seriousness and the sadness of a grave situation. It is this literary device which the evangelists use here.

The ninth hour is the hour of death; in dying Jesus utters a loud cry, which astonished those who were standing around: "And at the ninth hour Jesus cried with a loud voice, 'Eloi, Eloi, lama sabachthani,' which means, 'My God, My God, why hast thou forsaken me?' " (Mk 15:34–35). Jesus used Hebrew words, the first words of Ps 22. Both Mark and Matthew transcribe the

Hebrew into Greek letters and then translate them. Jesus, at the moment of death, turns to prayer, praying the psalm in Hebrew, the liturgical language of the time. It must have been in a liturgical context, otherwise Jesus would have used the Aramaic.

The meaning of this psalm should be closely reviewed. It is evident that the psalm is the long lament of an individual. Verses 2–22 describe the terrible situation of the individual who can turn only to God for help. Verses 23–32 are a hymn of the individual and can only be thanksgiving to God for the answer which God has given to this individual.

The Meaning and Themes of Psalm 22

There are two themes throughout Psalm 22. The first theme concerns the misery of the individual who is abandoned by friends, sick, and menaced by death in solitude. The second theme deals with hope in recourse to God alone, who can help him but who seems to do nothing to help the man in his anguish. God is silent but this does not stop the man from praying for aid. He knows that God has helped the chosen people before and thus he puts all his hope in God. "My God, my God, why hast thou forsaken me? Why art thou so far from helping me, from the words of my groaning? O my God, I cry by day, but thou dost not answer; and by night, but find no rest" (v. 1–2). "My God" is a classical liturgical expression of the alliance. That is why Yahweh can be directly addressed as "My" God. Moreover, God does not seem to answer his prayer.

Hope is depicted in (v. 3–5): "Yet thou art holy, enthroned on the praises of Israel. In thee our fathers trusted; they trusted, and thou didst deliver them." Yahweh himself is the firm and first foundation of his hope. He does not doubt God because of Israel's history in which God has so often intervened with mercy and love. They were never disappointed; Yahweh has heard his people in the past with the consequent assurance that it will take place again.

"But I am a worm, and no man; scorned by men, and despised by the people. All who see me mock at me, they make mouths at me, they wag their heads; 'He committed his cause to the Lord; let him deliver him, let him rescue him, for he delights in him!' " (v. 6–8). We have here the perfect description of a man who is all alone before the abuse and mercy of his enemies. It is like the condition of Jesus on the cross. Hope is again renewed: "Yet thou art he who took me from the womb; thou didst keep me safe upon my mother's breasts. Upon thee was I cast from my birth, and since my mother bore me thou hast been my God" (v. 9–10). This is the second affirmation of confidence in God, which is now based on the personal experience of the individual who is praying to God. Yahweh has been present to him as a father who has adopted him and has been a guide to him.

We have, below, a full description of the sufferings of an individual threatened by death:

> Be not far from me, for trouble is near and there is none to help. Many bulls encompass me, strong bulls of Bashan surround me; they open wide their mouths at me, like a ravening and roaring lion. I am poured out like water, and all my bones are out of joint; my heart is like wax, it is melted within by breast; my strength is dried up like a potsherd, and my tongue cleaves to my jaws; thou dost lay me in the dust of death. Yea, dogs are round about me; a company of evildoers encircle me; they have pierced my hands and feet—I can count all my bones—they stare and gloat over me; they divide my garments among them, and for my raiment they cast lots (v. 11–18).

The similarity of this description to those of Jesus on the cross is striking. For this reason, Christians adopted it very early as their own in reference to the passion.

The Lord is petitioned in verses 19–21: "But thou, O Lord, be not far off! O thou my help, hasten to my aid! Deliver my soul from the sword, my life from the power of the dog! Save me from the mouth of the lion, my afflicted soul from the horns of the wild oxen!"

It was common in Jewish literature to refer to one's enemies as "dogs," since in the East, dogs were held in disrepute. This petition was not in vain. He will receive a response in the second section of the psalm:

> I will tell of thy name to my brethren; in the midst of the congregation I will praise thee: You who fear the Lord, praise him! all you sons of Jacob, glorify him, and stand in awe of him, all you sons of Israel! For he has not despised or abhorred the affliction of the afflicted; and he has not hid his face from him, but has heard, when he cried to him. From thee comes my praise in the great congregation; my vows I will pay before those who fear him. The afflicted shall eat and be satisfied; those who seek him shall praise the Lord! May your hearts live for ever! (v. 22–26.)

The whole situation in the second half has radically changed. The supplicant's prayer has been answered and he now sings the praises of God.

This psalm was a primitive one, dating back to the fourth century B.C. It seems, however, that verses 27–31 are a later addition. They present evidence of a later eschatology: the whole earth will now praise God—not just the poor individual whom we have read about at the beginning of the psalm. This cosmic dimension of salvation is eschatological and messianic. It reads:

> All the ends of the earth shall remember and turn to the Lord; and all families of the nations shall worship before him. For dominion belongs to the Lord, and he rules over the nations. Yea, to him shall all the proud of the earth bow down; before him shall bow all who go down to the dust, and he who cannot keep himself alive. Posterity shall serve him; men shall tell of the Lord to the coming generation, and proclaim his deliverance to a people yet unborn, that he has wrought it (v. 27–31).

The evolution of this psalm appears to coincide with the theme of the suffering servant of Yahweh. Israel, by sharing in the suffering of the Messiah, would also share in his glory in messianic times and would aid in assembling all the families of the earth before God. There are many such allusions in Isaiah and Zechariah. The Jews of the second and first century B.C. certainly understood this psalm in the context of a Messiah who was also a suffering servant.

The New Testament has two uses for this psalm. It was used by Jesus himself as well as by the primitive Christian community. Jews and early Christians were well acquainted with the psalms as being somewhat of a resumé of the whole Bible. The psalms were their prayers and thus were used more often than any other part of the Bible. They also were used frequently in the liturgy and thus were very familiar. Psalm 22, which Mark puts in the mouth of Jesus on the cross, pertained to the Messiah, but in what way? Actually none of the many interpretations given to this text in Mk 15:34 is very helpful. What is clear is that we are confronted here by the great mystery of the suffering of the Son of God.

Albert Camus in *The Fall* says that Jesus lost his faith on the cross. According to Camus, Jesus would have been afflicted all of his life for having caused the death of the innocent children of Bethlehem. Camus believes that Jesus finally decided to die not to defend himself but because he chose not to be the only one of the innocent not to die. The cry of Jesus, therefore, was one of rebellion and shows that Jesus was not superhuman.

No serious exegete would accept such a theory or anything faintly resembling it. It is true that some form of abandonment did occur on the cross. Jesus was abandoned by disciples and friends, but he was not abandoned by God. God indeed does not intervene on behalf of Jesus in order to save him. The only sign would come later in the resurrection. But Jesus had to live out (and die) the whole human situation of solitude and suffering, of abandonment, to the bitter end. He was a man to the very end "in everything except sin," including death.

The whole Christian mystery of the Incarnation depends on this fact and was so understood by the early Christians. This does not follow human logic, which would have God intervene in his favor. It was exactly this challenge that was raised by the crowd and chief priests around the cross. Not even the disciples understood at first this mystery of the passion of Jesus. There was no miracle, and Jesus died as every man must die. Yet, if a miracle had occurred, that power would have been minor and of no lasting import, and Jesus simply would have assumed his former condition. It was only the resurrection which could inaugurate the new life, the new eon, a condition which is entirely different from the former life. But this resurrection could occur only after the real death of Jesus. There can be no new life without the death of the former. The resurrection was God's answer to the prayer of Jesus and a fuller sign than any miraculous descent from the cross. Once we have seen and understood the resurrection, the meaning of the passion can be understood.

There are, then, two aspects to the prayer of the psalm by Jesus on the cross. Jesus lived the human condition fully, as all men before and after him must do. Like them, he cried out in human anguish, loneliness, and seeming abandonment to God, his Father, for deliverance from the evil of death.

There was no miraculous intervention which could be seen by human eyes. Jesus made the words of the poor man of the psalm his own. He did this in his own anguish and trustful prayer to God, his Father. He had confidence in God in the face of suffering and death. In order to emphasize this, Luke adds a citation from Ps 30:6: "Into your hands I commend my spirit." Jesus in his passion was not some sort of actor playing a role. Jesus was a man who really knew the suffering and solitude of a fearful and dreading man. Jesus then really tasted death, but he believed even in death that God would not abandon him. The words of Ps 22 in the mouth of Jesus are not words of despair but of distress in the face of death; at the same time they are words of confidence in God. Jesus was faithful to God to the very end. The answer and response of God to this faith was the resurrection of Jesus.

The Reaction of the Bystanders

From Mark, it is evident that those around Jesus do not understand what he is saying since he is speaking in Hebrew:

"And some of the bystanders hearing it said, 'Behold, he is calling Elijah.' And one ran and, filling a sponge full of vinegar, put it on a reed and give it to him to drink, saying, 'Wait, let us see whether Elijah will come to take him down' " (Mk 15:36). They mistake "Eloi" (God) for Elijah, who was expected to return during eschatological times. They misunderstood the meaning of the whole event which was transpiring before their very eyes. Moreover, someone tried to alleviate the suffering of Jesus by giving him some vinegar or dry wine.

The final act of Jesus, before death, is to give forth a great cry (Mk 15:37). This aspect of the death of Jesus became traditional in Christian literature. Hence we read in the epistle to the Hebrews: "For Jesus, in the days of his earthly life, with a loud cry and tears, offered up prayers and supplications to him who was able to save him from death and was heard because of his reverent submission. And he, Son as he was, learned obedience from the things that he suffered; and when perfected, he became to all who obey him the cause of eternal salvation, called by God a high priest according to the order of Melchisedech" (5:7-10).

Some critics have claimed that it is not physiologically possible to cry out when one is on a cross. Thus the cry would be more of a sign of the freedom of Jesus at the very moment of death, and all the evangelists point out this perfect freedom of Jesus. John emphasizes this strongly: "When Jesus had tasted the vinegar, he said, 'It is consummated.' And bowing his head, he gave up his spirit" (Jn 19:30). Actually, the exact opposite would have had to happen if it were not so: one gives up the spirit, and then the head comes down. But Jesus is in complete control of his death. He does not die because of the suffering, he dies because he wants to die. That is why, later, Pilate wonders how Jesus could have died so soon. Pilate did not understand that Jesus died freely.

The events after the death of Jesus are depicted by Mark: "And the curtain of the temple was torn in two, from top to bottom. And when the centurion who stood facing him, saw that he thus breathed his last, he said, 'Truly this man was the Son of God!' " (Mk 15:38-39). The temple veil was a curtain which separated the Holy of Holies from the rest of the temple. This tearing shows that the temple has now lost its function. The old temple has now been replaced by the new temple, which is the resurrected body of Jesus. The old economy has lost its meaning and a new alliance, or covenant, has been established by God in Jesus.

The words of the centurion show that he was struck either by the way in which Jesus died or by his whole attitude during the passion. The observation is striking since, for the Jews, the death of Jesus was a sign of God's total abandonment of Jesus and his doctrine. For the centurion, however, it was just the opposite. He recognizes in Jesus a divine power, one united to God.

It seems that Mark obtained most of his information concerning the death of Jesus from the women who were eyewitnesses of these events: "There were also women looking on from afar, among whom were Mary Magdalene, and Mary the mother of James the younger and of Joses, and Salome, who, when he was in Galilee, followed him, and ministered to him; and also many other women who came up with him to Jerusalem" (15:40-41). The disciples had fled and only these women remained. Mark cites their names since they were the only eyewitnesses of the crucifixion, and also because he is preparing for what is to follow in the resurrection (16:1). They who were faithful to the end would be the first to see the resurrection.

Matthew gives us some extraordinary events which happened after the death of Jesus: "And behold, the curtain of the temple was torn in two, from top to bottom; and the earth shook, and the rocks were split; the tombs also were opened, and many bodies of the saints who had fallen asleep were raised, and coming out of the tombs after his resurrection they went into the holy city and appeared to many" (27:51-53). This whole passage was inspired by the fact that the death of Jesus inaugurated a new era, the new eon of the resurrection. One of the effects of this new era was the resurrection of the saints. It is unlikely that dead persons actually came back to life and were seen all over Jerusalem. Only Matthew mentions this.

In 1 Peter 3:19, the same treatment can be found: "Put to death in the flesh, he was brought to life in the spirit, in which he went to those spirits that were in prison." This is the same reference as is made in the Apostles' Creed. The meaning—after the literary form has been cleared away—is that the death of Jesus also affects those who are already dead, not simply those who are to follow Jesus. It is Jesus who gives life to all, both the living and the dead.

Resumé of the Passion

The preaching of the passion was an essential part of the Christian *kerygma*, of the good news of salvation insofar as it introduced the good news of the resurrection (cf. 1 Cor 15:3–8). St. Paul calls this the gospel he had received which all of the Apostles preached: "For I delivered to you as of first importance what I also received, that Christ died for our sins in accordance with the scriptures, that he was buried, that he was raised on the third day in accordance with the scriptures, and that he appeared to Cephas, then to the twelve."

The resurrection was always inseparable from the passion of Jesus in all of the *kerygma* of the Gospels, Acts of the Apostles, and the epistles. The resurrection of Jesus cannot be separated from his death. The historicity of the passion must be a fact under pain of destroying the Christian message. The apostles announce the passion and death of Jesus in exactly the same way as their Jewish adversaries. However, the disciples insist on the resurrection of Jesus and both are proclaimed as facts, one incomprehensible without the other.

The great task for the apostles was to explain the meaning of these events. If Jesus died and rose, he could not be like any other man who dies and remains dead. In order to understand this, the disciples of Jesus meditated on the words of Jesus and the Scriptures, particularly the theme of the suffering servant of Isaiah 53. The Jews had not been fully able to understand this theme. For the disciples, the resurrection is God's reply to the prayer of Jesus at death. As a matter of fact, this passion and death narrative formed the nucleus of the Gospels; only gradually were the other episodes of the Gospel, such as the public life of Jesus, introduced to the passion and resurrection narratives. There is an evolution in the Christian *kerygma*. First, there is a narration of the bare facts enlightened by the theology of the suffering servant. These perspectives are gradually expanded, by inclusion of the Last Supper, the anointing at Bethany, the betrayal, the joyous entrance into Jerusalem. This whole development is possible only because of the resurrection itself. The disciples believed that they were living in relationship to the Christ who had risen. This can be seen in the chief characteristics of each of the evangelists.

Mark. This evangelist integrates the narration of the passion into his whole Gospel. It is not isolated but its mention is made throughout the whole Gospel. Mark was faithful to the original *kerygma* but added some personal details that he knew (the man who fled naked in Gethsemane, the reference to the family of Simon of Cyrene and to Joseph of Arimathea, who dared to ask Pilate for the body of Jesus).

Mark distinguishes between two phases in the passion: the secret passion (the Last Supper, the garden) and the public passion (the arrest and death). The Last Supper could also be called his sacramental passion since during the meal Jesus pronounced the words of the passion over the bread and wine, which was his commitment to suffer his passion. Jesus' words of consecration are the promise of his will to give meaning to the coming events. The bread and wine become a double sign and symbol of the same reality: his life given for us. When the disciples commemorate the Last Supper, as Jesus asked, they will commemorate his sacrifice. Later in the passion Jesus will be silent; here he says, "This is my body, this is my blood." The agony in the garden is not simply an introduction to the passion or an exhortation to Christians; it is the prayer of Jesus to his Father. The hour of Jesus has come and his prayer makes him decide to take this passion upon himself and to effect the redemption.

The public passion of Jesus in the Gospel of Mark is narrated in a simple fashion and with candor. Mark presents very frankly the solitude and the humiliation of Jesus in his suffering and death. Jesus speaks only to proclaim that he is to the Sanhedrin the Messiah and to Pilate that he is king. The narrative is loyal with no effort to attenuate. He emphasizes that Jesus is the servant of God, totally committed to the will of God, who does not miraculously intervene on behalf of Jesus. Mark's juxtaposition of the torn veil and the confession of the centurion is important. The torn veil symbolizes that the old economy was destroyed by the death of Jesus. The centurion is a sort of spokesman for the pagans who would be the beneficiaries of the new economy. It is the act of faith in Jesus crucified and resurrected—like that of the centurion—which alone matters before God. In his sufferings, Jesus is the innocent servant of God. Thus the whole Gospel of Mark is a call to faith in the death and resurrection of Jesus.

Matthew. The passion account in Matthew has some additional details, but it follows Mark in its general contours. One can see this in the story of Judas. Matthew tells us how much Judas received for betraying Jesus, but this was probably done so as to cite the text from Zechariah 11:12: "If it seems right to you, give me my wages; but if not, keep them! and they weighed out as my wages thirty shekels of silver." There are also the details about the death of Judas, whom Matthew calls a "traitor." This preoccupation with Judas shows that the Gospel was directed to those who were already Christians since they wanted to know more details of the events. Judas knew and betrayed Jesus. He is like the Christian who knows and betrays Jesus— especially since they both participated in the Eucharist.

Another detail in Matthew concerns the dream of the wife

of Pontius Pilate. Yet all these details add almost nothing to the essential narration of the passion. The real distinctive characteristics of his Gospel are at the theological level.

Matthew goes further than Mark in his citations of Old Testament texts. Even his linguistic expression is biblical because of the allusions it evokes (cf. Mt 26:3–4 and Ps 30:14; Mt 26:15 and Zech 11:12–13; Mt 27:46 and all of Ps 22).

The author does not change anything which he has received from Mark but pushes his reflections further than does Mark. Thus Mt 26:1: "When Jesus had finished all these sayings, he said to his disciples, 'You know that after two days the Passover is coming, and the son of man will be delivered up to be crucified!' " This corresponds to Mk 14:1: "It was now two days before the Passover and the feast of the unleavened bread." The light in which Matthew places this event is similar to that of the death of Moses. The verse clearly tells us that Jesus knew clearly beforehand the events which were to befall him.

Three things are told to us: Jesus is the Son of Man of whom Daniel speaks; Jesus is the suffering servant referred to by Isaiah; and lastly, by relating Jesus' death to the Passover, Matthew gives it a sacrificial character. Jesus is the new victim of the new Pasch.

Another characteristic of Matthew's Gospel is his frequent use of the name of Jesus. Still another is that Matthew presents Jesus as the master of his passion at all times. "The Master says, 'My time is at hand' " (Mt 26:18). During the Last Supper Jesus told his disciples that one of them will betray him and Judas asks if it is he. Jesus answers: "You have said so" (Mt 26:25). Matthew is here indicating the complete foreknowledge of Jesus of all the events of the passsion.

When Jesus is in the garden, Matthew writes: "He fell on his face and prayed" (Mt 26:39). This depicts a liturgical attitude of prayer, not the humiliating fall on the ground of Mark (14:35). Matthew pictures Jesus adoring and praying to his father calmly and freely. The description of his prayer is not so brutally poignant as it is in Mark. Matthew also insists on using the term

"Christ" throughout the trial, as Jesus is being insulted and beaten. While he reports the passion faithfully, Matthew is careful to emphasize that Jesus knows all and that he is in complete control of the situation.

Finally, Matthew underlines the fact that the passion implies the rejection of Israel, and he stresses the responsibility of the Jews.

Matthew writes for those who are already Christians and his account was meant to be read in the liturgical community, calling on them to adore the Son of God. The words of the centurion are not so much a profession of faith, as they were in Mark, as an act of adoration caused by all those things surrounding the death of Jesus. "When the centurion and those who were with him saw the earthquake and what took place, they were filled with awe and said, 'Truly, this was the Son of God!' " (Mt 27:54.) The bystanders perceive the presence of God in the human suffering of Jesus.

Luke. This evangelist follows the common tradition of the other two Synoptics, but he had another source as well—perhaps of the whole passion. Luke gives us some new details but he also eliminates whatever seems artificial, illogical or minute in Mark's description. For example, Luke reports only one trial before the Sanhedrin and the night trial is not mentioned.

Luke —writing mostly for pagan converts—lessens the responsibility of Pilate in the death of Jesus and emphasize the role of the Jews. The evolution of Christian tradition is present here since the early Christians accentuated the guilt of the Jews and diminished that of the Romans. This is manifest even more in the Gospel of John—and yet, both Jews and Romans share some responsibility. The guilt of the Jews was accentuated because they were the chosen people who should have understood the design of God for his people but did not. A second cause of this might have been the persecution of the early Christians at the hands of the Jews—an unconscious type of polemic. Historically, both Jews and Romans were responsible for the death of

Jesus. Jesus forgives all: "Father, forgive them for they know not what they do" (Lk 23:34). And the disciple must follow the example of Jesus. Luke also emphasizes that the Christian must be associated with the passion of Jesus. This is the clear moral drawn from the story of Simon.

Another characteristic of his account is the theme that the passion is a violent confrontation between Jesus and the power of the devil. Luke concludes the temptation in the desert by saying: "And when the devil had ended every temptation, he departed from him until an opportune time" (4:13).

The word for this "time" is the Greek *kairos*, and when Luke begins the passion, he recalls the theme: "Then Satan entered into Judas called Iscariot. . . . So he . . . sought an opportunity [*kairos*] to betray him" (22:3, 6). The influence of Satan is revealed again in 22:31: "Simon, Simon, behold Satan has demanded to have you, that he might sift you like wheat." But Satan has no power over Peter because Jesus prays for him. And again the *kairos* is mentioned in 22:53: "This is your hour [*kairos*] and the power of darkness." The passion is seen as a combat with Satan, which ends with the victory of Jesus.

The innocence of Jesus is another characteristic of Luke's gospel. Pilate himself declares it: "I find no crime in this man" (23:4). As if to emphasize this, Pilate makes this statement twice. Jesus' innocence is implied by the women who weep for him on the road to Golgotha (23:35), as does the repentant thief. The testimony of the centurion is clear: "Certainly this man was innocent" (23:47). Finally, even the people who witnessed the death of Jesus had to admit their fault: "When they saw what had taken place, they returned home beating their breasts" (23:48). We may conclude by saying that Luke makes Christ the proto-type of the suffering and persecuted Christian. Luke calls us to imitate the suffering Christ.

John. This Gospel seems to give us its own synthesis since John takes liberty with regard to his sources. There are real differences between John and the Synoptics. John's style is more simple, and the discourse of the Last Supper summarizes his teachings. Immediately after the final words to his chosen apostles, John has Jesus go almost directly to trial.

The passion of Jesus is fully integrated into the whole of the Fourth Gospel. The trial and arrest are all vastly shortened to integrate the passion into the whole Gospel. The real trial for John was during the whole of Christ's life. John indicates this in the episode when Jesus was in Jerusalem for the Feast of the Dedication. The Jews thought he was blasphemous because he claimed God as his Father (10:22–33). Although they tried to stone him, in reality they had decided already to put him to death after he raised Lazarus from the dead (11:47–53). That is why John does not emphasize the trial as do the other Synoptics. The trial by the Jews had already taken place, and it was only a question of carrying out the sentence. The whole public life of Jesus was a trial in which some accepted and others rejected belief in him. It is this which will lead to Christ's death. Whoever does not believe in Jesus must believe that he is blaspheming and therefore deserves to die. It was those men as a group who refused to believe Jesus when he said, "I and the Father are one" (10:30), who came to the conclusion that Jesus must indeed die

It is also evident that in John's account the small details which show the humiliation and solitude of Jesus have disappeared. Simon of Cyrene is not mentioned and Jesus carries the cross himself. There is no mention of robbers, only of two men who were crucified with him. There is no mockery of Jesus while he is on the cross, nor does Jesus cry out the prayer of the 22d Psalm.

John's only preoccupation is to show us the liberty of Jesus during the passion and death. This establishes the kingdom of Jesus on earth. John does use the text of Scripture which shows that they are fulfilled in Jesus. The passion is seen (as in Luke) as a combat between the forces of evil and Jesus (darkness and light). This is even clearer in John. After Judas leaves to betray

Jesus, John remarks that "it was night" (13:30). The combat will end in the victory of the truth.

Even more strongly than Matthew, John emphasizes Jesus' foreknowledge of all the events which were to befall him. Israel also refuses to accept Jesus and in this lay Israel's rejection. The confrontation can be completed only by the death of Jesus on the cross. Jesus predicts this death on the cross at the very beginning of his public life (2:18). This was announced in the Scriptures, and they were fulfilled by these events of the passion, events predicted by Jesus.

John continuously stresses the fact that he was an eyewitness of the events he narrates, especially of the passion and death. He was at the foot of the cross. And after the soldier pierces the side of Jesus with a sword, John says: "He who saw it has borne witness, his testimony is true, and he knows he tells the truth" (19:35). John prefaces his passion narrative with an insight into the fundamental meaning of the event: "Now before the feast of the Passover, when Jesus knew that his hour had come to depart out of this world to the Father, having loved his own who were in the world, he loved them to the end" (13:1). It is this departure to the Father which gives the passion such a profound meaning. This departure—and the passion—is brought about by love so that in reality the passion of Jesus is the supreme manifestation of the love of Jesus for men.

Throughout the Gospel text, John is continuously unveiling for us the power and majesty of Jesus and his exaltation in glory, in which he is established by his whole life, but particularly by his passion and death. This theme of the glory and kingship of Jesus is clear in the triumphal entry of Jesus into Jerusalem. It becomes clearer during his dialogue with Pilate during the passion. In reality, it is Jesus who is the judge—not Pilate. Pilate unconsciously recognizes this when he exclaims to the Jews: "Shall I crucify your king?" (14:15.) It reappears in the inscription written by Pilate for the cross of Jesus. John strongly emphasizes this when he says: " 'Now is the judgment of this world, now shall the ruler of this world be cast out; and I, when I am lifted up from the earth, will draw all men to myself.' He said this to show by what death he was to die" (12:31–32).

The passion of Jesus renders judgment on the world. The use of the word "world" here means all that is evil. Jesus conquers evil and this conquest takes place when he is lifted up on the cross. This is his exaltation, or triumph. The cross is the place where Jesus completes his oblation of love, and at the same time it is the throne from which Jesus begins to exercise his royalty and manifest his glory.

6

The Resurrection and the
Empty Tomb

The resurrection of Jesus presents us with many problems. Not one of the apostles actually claims that he saw the resurrection of Jesus; in fact, no one ever claimed this. All the witnesses, however, do proclaim two things: that the tomb was empty and that they experienced various meetings with the living Jesus after he died. The Gospels give us a witness which is rather late in literary formulations, since the Gospel of Mark (the earliest canonical Gospel) was written after 60 A.D. much later than the preaching of the apostles. It is clear that the writings of the evangelists were not the sole basis of the Christian faith. Moreover, there are differences in the evangelical accounts of the resurrection. For instance, Mark and Matthew situate the first apparition in Galilee, whereas Luke and John place it in Jerusalem on the evening of the day Jesus arose. These Gospel texts simply do not supply enough information to provide a clear picture of the events of the resurrection as they actually took place.

In addition to the Gospels we have other testimonies to the resurrection, which we must also take into consideration, such as the account of Paul, the Acts of the Apostles, and the witness of the primitive Christian community. Before the Gospels were written, Christians believed and preached the reality of the resurrection of Jesus. The Gospels themselves must be situated in the framework of this primitive faith and preaching. This is the context in which the Gospels were written, and it will be of great value to study them.

The resurrection is a complicated reality. Moreover, the accounts of the resurrection employ a unique literary genre. Use of a unique genre was, indeed, necessary. Up to the resurrection we have been studying the human life of Jesus: a public life an arrest, a trial, a putting to death. This is similar to the story of many men before and after Jesus. The Gospels tell us that Jesus gives death a new meaning. We can even experience much of this in our own lives. However, when we enter into the realm of the resurrection we are in a region which escapes our experience and our history.

The resurrection of Jesus is not simply a return to a former life, as it was for Lazarus, for the daughter of Jairus, or for the son of the widow of Naim—all of whom had to die again. When the early Christians spoke of the resurrection of Jesus they meant that he really returned to life after death but that he no longer could exist as he did before. The humanity of Jesus has passed into a new state of being, which is radically different from that of ordinary human life. Yet this is beyond human experience and thus it is most difficult—if not impossible—to describe the reality of this event. There are some witnesses in the Gospels who claim that they have experienced this event, and they recount to us what they have experienced. It is for this reason that their testimony will have special features and characteristics.

The Ancient Confession of Faith

The faith of the early Christians was based totally on the fact that Jesus had risen from the dead and that this is attested to by witnesses. A perfect source for this confession of faith can be found in 1 Cor 15:3–11 and in the Acts of the Apostles. The text of Paul is in the context of a discussion of the possibility of a resurrection, since some of the Christians at Corinth had died and some believed that they would not rise again. The body was destroyed after death; hence how was it possible to rise again? Plato's idea of the survival of the soul (it was immortal because it was "spiritual") had some influence on this sentiment.

In this philosophical view, the body was not necessary for eternal life. Therefore a resurrection of the body was not necessary or even desirable. Paul exposes the problem in 15:35–36: "But some one will ask, 'How are the dead raised? With what kind of a body do they come?' You foolish man! What you sow does not come to life unless it dies." Paul's response is threefold. In the first part of the chapter (v. 1–11) he insists on the fact of the resurrection of Jesus, which has been attested to by a whole series of witnesses. In v. 12–34 he gives us the relationship between the resurrection of Jesus and the resurrection of the disciples. Jesus begins in his own humanity what will be in the humanity of all of his disciples at the end of time. Finally, in v. 35–58, Paul explores the philosophical question of what the resurrection will mean for our spirits. In addition, he explores the question of the resurrection of all Christians at the *Parousia.*

The reaction of Paul to the problem of the possibility of the resurrection is that the resurrection of Jesus is a fact attested to by witnesses; therefore, there is no question about its possibility for the disciples.

In the very first verses of this chapter, Paul gives us his message, the good news *(evanglion)*, which brings us happiness and peace. He preached this to the Corinthians:

> For I delivered to you as of first importance what I also received, that Christ died for our sins in accordance with the scriptures, that he was buried, that he was raised on the third day in accordance with the scriptures, and that he appeared to Cephas, then to the twelve. Then he appeared to more than five hundred at one time, most of whom are still alive, though some have fallen asleep. Then he appeared to James, then to all the apostles. Last of all, as to one untimely born, he appeared also to me. . . . Whether then it is I, or they, so we preach and so you believed (1 Cor 15:3–8, 11).

The first thing one notes is that Paul does not base his teaching on his own experience, but in union with the others of the apostolic community. Thus for Paul and the apostles, the personal experience of the resurrection does not suffice; the most important is the witness of the whole Church. That one person saw Jesus does not thereby authenticate his witness. It must be the witness of the whole Church, the collective tradition of the Church. It must be, as Paul phrases it, "What I have received."

Paul's verses comprise some fundamental facts: (1) Christ died for our sins, according to the Scriptures; (2) He was buried; (3) He has been raised to life, on the third day, according to the Scriptures; (4) He was seen by Peter, by the twelve, by five hundred brothers at one time, by James, by all the Apostles, and by Paul.

The subject of the whole message is Christ who died, was buried, and rose. That Christ died *for our sins* gives us the theological evaluation of this death, which we can understand only through the Scriptures. The detailed list of those who were actual witnesses to the resurrection of Jesus shows that these Christians considered the resurrection as a fact experienced by those members of the community. It is this fact which the entire community proclaims.

A literary examination of the text confirms Paul's testimony that he is handing down the tradition of the church. In 1 Cor 15:3–8 there is a series of expressions which Paul does not usually adopt in his writings. For instance, in v. 3 we read "Christ died for our sins" *(hamartión)*. Paul usually uses this word in the singular *(hamartia)*, not in the plural. In v. 5, 6, 7, and 8 the Greek text reads: "he was seen" *(ophthè)*. Paul normally uses the word *apokalypsis*, which means appearance or revelation, rather than the word "seeing." In v. 5 the text says that Christ was seen by the twelve *(dodeka)*.

In all of Paul's writings he speaks only of *apostoloi* (apostles), not *dodeka*. Likewise, the expression "according to the Scriptures" is not a part of Paul's usual vocabulary. All these indications would point to the fact that Paul was not seeking to set forth his own personal views in this section of his epistle but simple was quoting something he had learned by heart, on which he based his theology and preached to the Corinthians. In 1 Cor 15:3–8 we have, therefore, a resumé of the official faith confession of the primitive Church.

How ancient is this confession of faith? Paul writes that he was taught this confession, and that he himself then taught the Corinthians. We know that in Acts 18:11–12 Paul was working in Corinth for a year and a half during the time of the Roman governor Gallio. We also know that this Roman, who was the brother of Seneca, was governor of Corinth about the year 50 A.D. It follows that since Paul had received the confession before, it must have been composed earlier. Paul received his Christian initiation around the year 36, in Damascus, and was baptized there (Acts 9:10–19). It is logical to suppose that he received this confession of faith at this time.

The text itself proclaims the same message found in the Acts of the Apostles. The emphasis of the whole confession is upon these words: "he was raised [*egeigertai*]on the third day, according to the Scriptures." The word *egeigertai* is ambiguous in that it can be translated "he was raised" or "he raised himself." The early Christians usually interpreted this to mean that "he was raised" since it was the Father who raised Jesus from the dead. The other alternative would not express this nuance clearly enough.

The expression "on the third day" referred to the fact of burial, perhaps to signify that Jesus rose very quickly or to signify that he fulfilled a scriptural prophecy by his resurrection. It is difficult to find an earlier scriptural reference to this event. Perhaps the following text was in the mind of the early Christians: "Come, let us return to the Lord; for he was torn, that he may heal us; he was stricken, and he will bind us up. After two days he will revive us; on the third day, he will raise us up, that we may live before him" (Hosea 6:1–2). This text, however, refers to a penitential liturgy in which sinful Israelites returned to Yahweh. After a short time of penance, God will raise them up again by pardoning their sins. Perhaps the early Christians included this in their liturgy and it is being alluded to in this confession of faith.

According to official Jewish law, a man was not dead until after three days. If this is so, then the expression "after three days" can mean the fact of the death of Jesus, as well as its short duration. The event of the resurrection was made more understandable for the disciples by referring to earlier texts of Scripture.

The confession emphasizes that the resurrected Jesus was seen by many people. It uses the Greek word *ophthae* ("to see"), which means an immediate experience in which the eyes play an essential role. It was a form of direct knowledge through sight. The word can also mean "to meet." It does not mean to contemplate *(theorein)* or to meet mystically *(blepein).* When the confession says that Jesus was seen by the disciples, the disciples mean that they really met him and saw him with their own eyes. The concreteness of the event was absolutely imperative for the Christian *kerygma.*

The people who saw Jesus are listed by the confession. None of them actually saw the resurrection itself, but only the risen Jesus, just as no one witnessed the creation, only its effects. They are witnesses to the result of God's creative work. This is what the confession of faith affirms. The witnesses are listed in the order of their authority as witnesses. The most important are "Cephas and the twelve," and Peter has a special place in this group. Jesus was seen first by Peter alone, and only afterward was he seen by the other twelve. The confession then mentions the group of five hundred brothers who saw Jesus at once *(ephapax).* Then he was seen by James and all the apostles, all of whom hold secondary places alongside Peter and the twelve. This presents a difficulty since we usually identify "the twelve" with "the apostles." Was there a difference?

It is evident from the text of the confession that certain people were considered to be apostles without being part of "the twelve." Luke claims that only the twelve are apostles (Acts), but Paul loudly claims that he too is an apostle. They who have seen the risen Lord, and they alone have the right to the title apostle, and yet the five hundred saw the risen Christ and do not have this title. Something more than having seen the risen Lord must be necessary.

Paul refers to himself as having "seen" *(ophthae)* the risen Lord as a last witness. We know this from Acts 9:1–8; 22:5–16; 26:12–18; and Gal 1:12–17. Yet this experience is different from that of the other twelve. In the Gospels, Jesus is with his disciples, he eats and sleeps with them, they touch his wounds. But when Paul describes his own vision, he uses the word *apokalypsis*. Jesus appears within a great light in the midst of which Jesus says, "Why do you persecute me?" (Acts 9:4.) Paul gives no description of the risen Lord and uses the word "apparition" to describe his meeting with Jesus.

We may conclude our study of this primitive confession of faith by saying that it is very primitive; its origin was probably in Palestine, affirming the resurrection of Jesus as the primordial event. It is attested to by having been experienced empirically, as a concrete fact. There was a whole series of persons who attested to this fact, and the community could name these persons who were then still alive. The decisive factor was not the personal witness of only one or the other, but the witness of the whole group together. This fact is given to us very simply, without the usual fantastic imagery used when describing ancient miracles. This same simplicity is present in the Acts of the Apostles.

The Acts of the Apostles

This book of the New Testament provides summaries of the preaching of the first Christians. They are very sober and simple, traits testifying to their antiquity.

The word "witness" *(martyr)* is perhaps the oldest word in this book that describes the activity of the disciples of Jesus after the resurrection. Just before the ascension Jesus gives his last reply to the disciples' question about the establishment of the kingdom: "But you shall receive power when the Holy Spirit has come upon you; and you shall be my witnesses in Jerusalem and in all Judea and Samaria and to the end of the earth" (1:8).

The idea is not that Jesus "sends" the apostles but that they are to be his witnesses. Therefore, the idea of witness is older than the idea of mission. As a result of their experience of the resurrection of Jesus and the power of the Holy Spirit, they will be the witnesses of Jesus to all men.

This is emphasized in Acts 1:21–22 as well: "One of the men who have accompanied us during all the time that the Lord Jesus went in and out among us, beginning from the baptism of John until the day when he was taken from us—one of these men must become with us a witness to his resurrection." The essential function of an apostle was to be a witness to the resurrection; but to be one of the twelve, the person had to have borne witness to the whole public life of Jesus as well.

The sermon of Peter on the first day of Pentecost bears evidence of this primitive teaching. Peter cites the prophet Joel (2:28–32) at some length. There are quotes from Ps 16:8–11 and Ps 110. These scriptural references show a degree of learning and research and were probably composed after the event; moveover, the references make sense only when they refer to the Greek translation of the Old Testament (LXX).

Peter gives us the essential elements of the faith: "Jesus of Nazareth, a man attested to you by God with mighty works and wonders and signs which God did through him in your midst, as you yourselves well know—this Jesus, delivered up according to the definite plan and foreknowledge of God, you crucified and killed by the hands of lawless men. But God raised him up" (Acts 2:22–24). And again: "This Jesus God raised up, and of that we are all witnesses. Being therefore exalted at the right hand of God, and having received from the Father the promise of the Holy Spirit, he has poured out this which you see and hear" (Acts 2:32–33).

We should notice that this witness in v. 32 is collective. It is not just personal on the part of Peter. The next verse (33) introduces a new idea to the primitive confession, namely, that Jesus has been exalted, thereby entering a higher state of being. Jesus is now completely and immediately associated with the royal power of God. Jesus, pictured as sitting at a throne, in power and "at the right hand of God," shares absolutely in God's power over the world. Jesus exists in a superior condition of existence, indeed in cosmic power. The Holy Spirit is given in the name of Jesus and by the power which his name evokes.

Peter again preaches to the Jews in Acts 3:12–26 after the cure of the lame beggar. While recalling the passion, Peter proclaims that God "glorified his servant Jesus, when you delivered him up and denied him" (3:13). Peter calls Jesus "the Holy and Righteous One," and "the Author of Life" (3:14–15). The expression "deliver up," which Peter uses here, is important; it refers to the suffering servant of Isaiah 53 and concludes (v. 13) that God "glorified" Jesus. In v. 15 he repeats the theme more clearly when he says: "To this we are all witnesses."

In all of this we see the very core of the Christian message preached to all men: Jesus who suffered was raised up by God, and all the apostles together testify to this fact. Nothing makes sense without the resurrection of Jesus (3:16).

We see an important resumé of the apostolic *kerygma* in Acts 5:30–32: "The God of our fathers raised Jesus whom you killed by hanging him on a tree. God exalted him at his right hand as leader and Saviour—to give repentance to Israel and forgiveness of sins. And we are witnesses to these things, and so is the Holy Spirit whom God has given to those who obey him." Thus the Father (the Greek has the article to designate God, the Father) has raised Jesus after the Jews have killed him. The resurrection is God's response and so God raised him up *(egeiro).*

Peter adds that God exalted him *(hypsosen,* "to uplift") or elevated his former condition. Peter also calls Christ leader *(archēgos)* and savior *(Sotēr).* By his resurrection and exaltation, Jesus is established as the leader or prince, or as one who is at the head of the line. He is also one who saves. His triumph came in being raised up, and this is the source of our salvation and the forgiveness of sins. The apostles were witnesses to all of these things with the Holy Spirit, who bears witness through them.

One final section from the Acts of the Apostles is Peter's sermon to the centurion Cornelius and his household. We have here a complete text: an introduction (10:34-55), and a resumé of the primitive catechesis. It started with the baptism of John (v. 37) since everything started at this point: "God anointed Jesus of Nazareth with the Holy Spirit and with power" (10:38). The anointing signifies that Jesus is the Messiah, or the Christ. Then Peter relates how Christ went about doing good (v. 37-39) and that the apostles were witnesses of this activity. Christ was then put to death: "But God raised him on the third day and made him manifest, not to all the people but to us who were chosen by God as witnesses, who ate and drank with him after he rose from the dead" (10:40-41).

We find here more details which are not to be found elsewhere. We have the first mention of "the third day" in the Acts. Second, the experience of the resurrection is not given to just anyone, as is knowledge of the public life of Jesus. It is given only to those witnesses whom God has specially prepared. There were some elected by God to be witnesses. Third, more concrete details are given: the expression "he ate and drank" is used for the first time. Peter concludes his sermon by saying that the apostles preach by the order of Jesus and that God has made him judge of the living and the dead, to whom all the prophets attested (v. 42-43).

Let us conclude our study of the Acts. The sermons contained therein are primitive, and they show us the power and miracles of Christ rather than his teaching. The disciples insist, above all, on the death and resurrection of Jesus. The details of this experience are given to us here: Jesus was raised *(egeiro)*, he was exalted *(hypsoo)* by the Father at his right hand so that now as resurrected Lord, Jesus is leader *(archēgos)* and Savior *(Sotēr)* and shares absolutely in the Father's power. Because of this power, Jesus can give the Holy Spirit and forgiveness of sins to those who believe and are converted. The essential function of the twelve is to give witness to all of this, chosen as they are for this task by God. Through their word, God offers salvation to all men. This message is presented soberly and simply, and this itself is a guarantee of its antiquity and truthfulness. Only in Acts 10:40–41 are we given any details beyond those given us in the confession of faith in 1 Cor 15:3–8. The early Christians made use of the Scripture apologetically in order to explain the meaning of the resurrection and exaltation of Jesus.

Influence of the Resurrection on the Primitive Community

The constant repetition of the fact of the resurrection is easily seen in the New Testament. The early Christians continuously recalled this event, which is the whole basis of the Christian life and belief. Indeed, as we have seen, the essential mission of the apostles is to bear witness to the Paschal mystery. But what of other aspects of the Christian life?

The Liturgy. The Christian liturgy can have no meaning whatever without the resurrection of Jesus within the perspective of the *Parousia*, or second coming of Christ. Christians commemorate the Last Supper by commemorating the death of Jesus. It is not simply a memorial, it is a death which effected redemption and leads to our own resurrection into the life of Jesus. The Eucharist places the Christian with the risen Christ until he comes at the *Parousia*. The awaiting of the second coming was so much a part of the mentality of the early Christians that they concluded all of their liturgical services with the prayer or invocation *Maranatha*, "Lord, come." This was retained in the original Aramaic in the New Testament.

The hymns of the New Testament also recall the resurrection and exaltation of Jesus: "Who, though he was in the form of God, did not count equality with God a thing to be grasped, but emptied himself, taking the form of a servant, being born in the likeness of man. And being found in human form he humbled himself and became obedient unto death, even death on a cross. Therefore God has highly exalted him and bestowed on him the name which is above every name, that at the name of Jesus every knee should bow. . . ." (Phil 2:6–10; cf. Col 1:15–20).

Morality. Without the resurrection, Christian morality is also meaningless. Christian morality is totally directed toward putting on the new man in Christ and growing in him. Christianity is a new life in the resurrected Christ, perfected in us by Christ.

Theology. Even if the Gospels were to give us no account of the resurrection, Christianity would still exist since there were still some men who declared that they had seen the risen Christ. They proclaimed that those who accepted Christ would experience the gift of the Holy Spirit with a living community of all those who accepted this essential message. The resurrection for the primitive Christian community was a fact; St. Paul never read any account of the resurrection but says simply that he had seen the risen Lord (cf. Acts 9:1–9; 22:5–16; 26:12–20; Gal 1:12–24; 1 Cor 9:1; 15:8–40). These men never claim to have seen an illumination or ghost: they declare the resurrection as a fact, an empirical fact of their experience that they *saw* the risen Lord.

What did the resurrection mean for these Christians? Jesus, first of all, did not simply return to his former human and public life. He was glorified and exalted above this former condition and became Lord (cf. Ps 110), sharing fully in the absolute power of the Father. The gift of the Holy Spirit to those who believe is a function of the eschatological kingdom of Christ. This exalted condition, or existence, of Jesus is radically different from any which we do or can experience, and that is why Christ did not appear to just anyone. For to perceive the risen Lord, a man must be specially prepared by God.

Paul and John both meditated on what the resurrection of Jesus meant for Christians. In his transformed humanity, Christ realizes in himself the state of being of all humanity at the end of time. Indeed, through the Holy Spirit, Jesus even now begins to make this eschatological existence real in Christians. In 1 Cor 15:36-44 Paul compares our present life to the growth of a grain of wheat into a plant. The time of full maturity is the resurrection, but there is a growth even during our lives now. There is a continuity between the seed, its growth, and its maturity. It is God who gives it growth toward maturity (1 Cor 15:38).

Paul compares the state of our present existence in Christ with that of the first existence. The first Adam is characterized by corruption, mortality, and ignorance. The heavenly second Adam will be incorruptible, immortal, and glorious. We will have a "spiritual body"—the full meaning of which we now cannot understand. We know that our bodies will be transformed because they are part of us, but exactly how this will be is a mystery (1 Cor 15:51).

John gives us some reflections on this as well: "See what love the Father has given us, that we should be called children of God, and so we are. The reason why the world does not know us is that it does not know him. Beloved, we are God's children now; it does not yet appear what we shall be, but we do know that when he appears we shall be like him, for we shall see him as he is. And every one who thus hopes in him purifies himself as he is pure" (1 Jn 3:1-3).

John uses no metaphor here, and we can know this reality only through faith since it cannot be seen or felt. The world— those who refuse God—does not know him. Christians know God and even now participate in the eschatological kingdom by the resurrection. What we shall fully be at the *Parousia* we do not as yet know; the only thing we do know is that we will be like the risen Lord. When we are like him we shall then—and only then—see him. We cannot see him completely now, because we are not as yet completely like him. Indeed, we are even now the children of God, and this knowledge comes to us by faith. But our knowledge is imperfect; through the Holy Spirit something of the resurrection of Jesus has begun in us now but has not as yet been brought to full perfection.

The Gospel Accounts of the Resurrection

It is evident from a cursory reading of each of the four Gospels that the passion is never given without the resurrection, which is the very climax of the passion narrations and of the Gospels themselves. Each of the Gospels divides the resurrection event into two phases: the discovery of the empty tomb (since no one was present when it actually became empty), and the Paschal experiences of the risen Lord with the disciples. This is how we shall divide our own presentation.

Mark.

And when the sabbath was past, Mary Magdalene and Mary the mother of James, and Salome, brought spices, so that they might go and anoint him. And very early on the first day of the week they went to the tomb when the sun had risen. And they were saying to one another, "Who will roll away the stone for us from the door of the tomb?" And looking up, they saw that the stone was rolled back; for it was very large. And entering the tomb, they saw a young man sitting on the right side, dressed in a white robe; and they were amazed. And he said to them, "Do not be amazed; you seek Jesus of Nazareth, who was crucified. He is risen, he is not here; see the place where they laid him. But go, tell his disciples and Peter that he is going before you to Galilee; there you will see him as he told you." And they went out and fled from the tomb; for trembling and astonishment had come upon them; and they said nothing to anyone, for they were afraid (16:1–8).

At the end of Chapter 15 (v. 42–43) Mark records that Joseph of Arimathea dared to ask Pilate for the body of Jesus for a decent burial. Jesus was wrapped in a linen shroud and buried in a tomb hollowed from a rock. A large stone, as was the custom, was placed at the entrance since tombs were considered the rooms of the dead.

The women who had followed Jesus came on the day after the Sabbath to embalm Jesus since there was no time for this on the day of his burial. When they arrived at the tomb, they found it empty and saw therein a young man in white. They were amazed. A characteristic of theophanies in the Bible is noted here when the young man tells them not to be afraid. The message is that of Christ's Paschal mystery. After recalling the passion and death of Jesus, the young man says, "He is not here," but has risen in triumph over death. The empty tomb is the negative sign of the resurrection.

The three women received a mission to go tell the disciples of this event (all the accounts of the resurrection give the disciples a mission to bear witness). Peter has a special place: "Go tell his disciples and Peter...." The young man mentions some form of promise which Jesus had made to the disciples to meet them in Galilee. The whole account is, once again, sober and simple.

The last verse (8) is striking because it does not really correspond with v. 5–7, where the young man tells them not to be afraid. This seems to be from another account of events which pictures the women fleeing from the empty tomb as if it had been desecrated, something which upsets them terribly. It also seems that the disciples had fled from Jerusalem to Galilee out of fear.

In retrospect, we see that the last verse (8) contrasts very forcefully with the preceding two verses. Probably the theophany of the young man is a later theological development; this would explain the empty tomb and its significance. If the Gospel had merely recorded that the women fled from the empty tomb, it could mean that someone had merely desecrated the tomb. Thus, catechetically it would be necessary to explain correctly the significance of the empty tomb. Theological reflection used the theophany of the young man to clarify that the empty tomb was a sign of the resurrection of Jesus.

Matthew.

> Now after the sabbath, toward the dawn of the first day of the week, Mary Magdalene and the other Mary went to see the sepulchre. And behold, there was a great earthquake; for an angel of the Lord descended from heaven and came and rolled back the stone, and sat upon it. His appearance was like lightning and his raiment white as snow. And for fear of him the guards trembled and became like dead men. But the angel said to the women, "Do not be afraid; for I know that you seek Jesus who was crucified. He is not here; for he has risen as he said. Come, see the place where he lay. Then go quickly and tell his disciples that he has risen from the dead, and behold, he is going before you to Galilee; there you will see him. Lo, I have told you." So they departed quickly from the tomb with fear and great joy, and ran to tell his disciples (28:1–8).

Matthew simplifies the human facts in his description of the empty tomb. He leaves out the mention of Salome. Yet he develops the theophany of the young man (v. 2–4): earthquake, the angel, the rolling back of the stone and the angel seated on it, the fear of the soldiers, his appearance like lightning. Thus Matthew uses the classical vocabulary of theophanies in the Bible. Matthew is the only evangelist to mention the soldiers at the tomb. They were placed there at the suggestion of the Jews (Mt 27:62–66). In Mt 28:5–7, mention is again made of the soldiers for apologetical reasons. The description is clearly related to conveying the idea that Jesus is risen and that as evidence of this we are told of the empty tomb. The two women also receive a mission to tell the other disciples, but Matthew gives Peter no special mention.

Luke.

> But on the first day of the week, at early dawn, they went to the tomb, taking the spices which they had prepared. And they found the stone rolled away from the tomb, but when

> they went in they did not find the body. While they were perplexed about this, behold, two men stood by them in dazzling apparel; and as they were frightened and bowed their faces to the ground the men said to them, "Why do you seek the living among the dead? Remember how he told you, while he was still in Galilee, that the Son of Man must be delivered into the hands of sinful men, and crucified, and on the third day rise." And they remembered his words, and returning from the tomb they told all this to the eleven and to all the rest. Now it was Mary Magdalene and Joanna and Mary the mother of James and the other women with them who told this to the apostles; but these words seemed to them an idle tale, and they did not believe them (24:1–11).

Concrete details in this account are missing. The names of the women are given only later in the account (v. 10). Luke claims that the women made the spices while Mark says they they bought them. Luke probably reasoned that since it was the Sabbath they must have made the spices earlier. The shops would have been closed on the Sabbath, and it was too early in the day to buy anything. Luke's theophany is more simple than that of Matthew, with the essential points brought out in v. 3: "But when they went in, they did not find the body."

The tone of the account changes in v. 4–8 when two dazzling men appear and the women are afraid. Luke is the only one who mentions two men; Mark says that there was one young man; Matthew mentions an angel. Luke's account of their words bids the women to "remember," that is, to understand the profound meaning of the words which Jesus had spoken. This theme of "remembering" will be very important in the account of John.

Finally, as in the other two accounts, the women are given the mission to announce this good news to the other disciples, and all fear has now disappeared from the women. Judas is no longer numbered among the twelve ("the eleven") and Luke is careful to distinguish the eleven from the rest of the apostles.

The essential message of each of these accounts is the fact that the tomb was empty, a point insisted on by the Christians.

The Jews never disputed that the tomb was empty—only how it got that way. This was a common accusation against the resurrection (e.g., see the defense of St. Justin in his *Dialogue with Tryphon*, pars. 132–135). Some argued that someone had stolen the body and deceived the apostles.

Several other explanations also are possible. The first argument about the theft of the body of Jesus can be defended. An empty tomb does not automatically lead to a conclusion of resurrection. This seems to be improbable, however, since respect for a dead body was very great in the ancient world. The argument that someone other than the apostles stole the body seems to lack credibility. Were it true, it would have been very easy for those who had stolen the body to refute the apostles when they started preaching the resurrection of Jesus.

In conclusion, the essential element of the empty tomb is that it is a sign. It is a sign that Jesus has risen; the mission of the women is to bear witness to this sign.

7

The Paschal Appearances

The Catholic Church considers the following verses from the Gospel of Mark to be inspired. However, it is doubtful whether it was Mark who wrote them. The passage is lacking in many ancient manuscripts.*

Mark.

Now when he rose early on the first day of the week, he appeared first to Mary Magdalene, from whom he had cast out seven demons. She went and told those who had been with him, as they mourned and wept. But when they heard that he was alive, and had been seen by her, they would not believe it. After this he appeared in another form to two of them as they sat at table; so he upbraided them for their unbelief and hardness of heart, because they had not believed those who saw him after he had risen. And he said to them, "Go into all the world and preach the gospel to the whole creation. He who believes and is baptized will be saved; but he who does not believe will be condemned. And these signs will accompany those who believe: in my name they will cast out demons; they will speak in new tongues; they will pick up serpents, and if they drink any deadly thing, it will not hurt them; they will lay their hands on the sick, and they will recover." So then the Lord Jesus, after he had spoken to them, was taken up into heaven, and sat

_____

* The RSV regards the passage as a non-canonical addition.

down at the right hand of God. And they went forth and preached everywhere, while the Lord worked with them and confirmed the message by the signs that attended it. Amen (16:9–20).

It is clear that Mark's Gospel ends abruptly at 16:8 after Mark has announced (v. 7) that Jesus would appear to the apostles in Galilee. Perhaps some other disciple added this section.

Matthew.

And behold, Jesus met them and said, "Hail." And they came up and took hold of his feet and worshiped him. Then Jesus said to them, "Do not be afraid; go and tell my brothers to go to Galilee, and there they will see me."

Now the eleven disciples went to Galilee, to the mountain to which Jesus had directed them. And when they saw him they worshiped him; but some doubted. And Jesus came and said to them, "All authority in heaven and on earth has been given to me. Go therefore and make disciples of all nations, baptizing them in the name of the Father and of the Son and of the Holy Spirit, teaching them to observe all that I have commanded you; and lo, I am with you always, to the close of the age" (28:9–10, 12–20).

Matthew is brief and has Jesus go to meet the women, taking the initiative himself in revealing himself. The greeting of Jesus, "Hail," can also mean "rejoice" since the Paschal mystery cannot inspire fear but only joy. In Matthew, the women take hold of the feet of Jesus as a sign of respect and worship. The women are given the mission to announce the good news and to direct the disciples to go to Galilee. The women play an important role in the Gospel narration, yet in the ancient confession of faith (1 Cor 15:3–8) they are not mentioned. The reason is that women were considered to be minors and could not juridically testify to anything. These women were in fact the first witnesses because they had been faithful to Jesus on the cross. If this had not happened historically, it would never have been recorded, since such a preference was not very flattering to the "twelve."

The rest (v. 16–20) gives us a concise account of the appearance of Jesus to his disciples in Galilee. They were only eleven since Judas had already been eliminated. The word used in the phrase "and when they *saw* him" *(horeo)* is the same word used in the confession of faith in 1 Cor 15:3-8.

Then Jesus gives the mission to the apostles. This last phrase of Jesus is very important.

All authority in heaven and earth has been given to me (v. 18). This reveals the final enthronement of Jesus in eschatological power, underlying the profound reality of the resurrection. By his resurrection, Jesus has entered into a royal condition in which he has universal cosmic power from God. It is in virtue of this that Jesus can give the following mission: "Go therefore and make disciples of all nations" (v. 19). The word "go" *(porenthentes)* means to walk, to walk to all nations of the world. We have here the universal mission of the apostles to all peoples and all nations. *Mathaiteusate* means "to make disciples," not "to teach," since Jesus had not come simply to teach but to draw all men to himself and make of them his disciples. The mission of the apostles is not simply to impart a doctrine but to give a life. They are to do so by baptism, to open men up to the power of God who is Father, Son, and Holy Spirit. It is not just to adhere to Jesus but to participate in the Spirit and thereby to recognize that all things come from the Father.

The Gospel of Matthew ends with a promise: "And lo, I am with you always, to the end of the age" (v. 20). Jesus can make such a promise because he is Lord and has royal power from God until the fulfillment of the present time in the final eschatological kingdom. The mission of the apostles is given by Jesus alone, and it can be realized only by living in communion with him each day until the end. The whole mission itself of the apostles is radically related to the resurrection of Jesus.

Here we have the profound consciousness of the primitive Church. We have here the resumé of the whole Gospel in a confession of faith which affirms that the disciples saw Jesus. They *saw* Jesus, not simply a vision. Jesus is Lord and his Lordship is the foundation of their very mission, which Jesus promises will endure until the end of time. It is the "present time" which is the mission of the Church. Jesus is alive and is Lord of the eschatological era, and the disciples have a mission to accomplish with Jesus since Jesus is with his disciples all days. The disciples, in reality, participate in this lordship and power of Jesus on earth.

Luke. Two appearances of Jesus after his resurrection are recounted by Luke, the first to the two disciples going to Emmaus (24:31-36) and the second to all the disciples in Jerusalem (24:36–53). After the women had announced the discovery of the empty tomb, Peter rose and ran to the tomb; stooping and looking in, he saw the linen cloths by themselves; and he went home wondering at what had happened (24:12).

Many authors claim that this phrase is not authentic. It is missing in many good manuscripts (e.g., Codex Bezae). Other authors think that verse 12 is a primitive memory which has some historical importance. It emphasizes that, although the rest were skeptical, Peter went to the tomb to see for himself. The state of Peter's mind is neither fear nor skepticism but wonder at this event for which he could find no explanation. It is possible that Peter could have witnessed a special appearance of Jesus since he was still in Jerusalem and Peter is mentioned separately in Lk 24:34, as well as in Mk 16:7. This would also explain why in 1 Cor 15:3 Peter is given a special place. All these independent sources seem to agree that Peter witnessed an appearance which is never recounted in the Gospels. The allusion of Luke is especially striking in view of the fact that when the two disciples return from Emmaus to Jerusalem (Lk 24:34), they are greeted by the news that Peter has seen Jesus alive, even before they could relate their own story. Luke does not give us the account; he presupposes it. Luke—and the other evangelists—did not wish, it seems, to recount all the appearances of the risen Lord.

Luke 24:36–53 gives us the last manifestation of the risen Jesus and the ascension, in which Jesus announces his return. If we compare it with Mt 28:16–20 we can note both similarities and differences. These can be seen most clearly if we arrange episodes in parallel columns.

MATTHEW	LUKE
On a mountain in Galilee	In Jerusalem
They saw him	He stood among them
Their reaction	Their reaction
worship	terror and fear
some doubt	joy and wonder
Jesus came	He eats, they touch him
He speaks	He speaks
v. 18: eschatological enthronment	v. 44: open their minds to understand the Scriptures
v. 19: universal mission	v. 45: event of the resurrection
v. 20: mission sustained by the Savior	v. 46: mission, proclaim the resurrection announce the forgiveness of sins

On the evening of Easter, after the two disciples returned from Emmaus, Jesus appears to them (24:36). The disciples can actually see him. The appearance of Jesus to his disciples after the resurrection is very simple. The reaction in Luke is that, at first, the disciples feared, and then their fear turned to joy. At first, the disciples think they are seeing a ghost, but they could touch him as one who had flesh and bones (v. 40–42), and he even eats with them.

Jesus now gives the disciples their mission:

Then he said to them, "These are my words which I spoke to you, while I was still with you, that everything written about me in the land of Moses and the prophets and the psalms must be fulfilled." Then he opened their minds to understand the scriptures, and said to them, "Thus it is written, that the Christ should suffer and on the third day rise from the dead, and that repentance and forgiveness of sins should be preached in his name to all nations, beginning from Jerusalem. You are witnesses to these things. And behold I send you the promise of my Father upon you: but stay in the city, until you are clothed with power from on high" (Lk 24:44–49).

Jesus opens the minds of the disciples to the fulfillment of the Scriptures concerning his passion and resurrection, giving them the ability to understand fully the inner meaning of these Scriptures. The Paschal mystery is that Jesus died and rose and that he accomplished the forgiveness of sins and conversion, which were to be preached to all the nations starting with Jerusalem.

The promise of Jesus in Luke is similar to that in Matthew (28:20). The promise is the Spirit, whom the disciples will receive to enable them to fulfill their mission.

The ascension of Jesus takes place almost immediately, with the impression that it took place almost on the same day. Acts situates it forty days later.

A comparison of Luke and Matthew is in order since they write about the same events. They both write very simply, without the element of the fantastic which characterized the ancient theophanies of the gods. In both accounts, the disciples see Jesus, and the reaction of the disciples is manifold: fear, wonder, joy. The fact that the disciples can touch Jesus and eat with him proves clearly that Jesus is alive again. Some (in Luke) did not believe, but this was natural. The disciples had nothing in their experience which could possibly prepare them for this event. In both evangelists there is the conferring of the mission. The transformation of Jesus in the resurrection is the source of this mission, which Jesus himself had not mentioned in his own public life. Thus the resurrection is the beginning of universal salvation. This resurrection is now experienced by the disciples.

John. Chapter 20 of the Gospel of John describes two ap-

pearances of the risen Christ to his disciples. The first appearance takes place in Jerusalem (20:11–18) on the evening of Easter.
John emphasizes that the first appearance of the risen Lord takes
place on the first day of the week (Sunday) and that the second
takes place eight days later (also Sunday). John's insistence on
Sunday appearances probably underlines the liturgical use of this
day (even as early as the first century). Sunday was already the
day of the Lord.

The narration of the first appearance of Jesus is simple:
Jesus comes into their midst. There is nothing extraordinary in
the appearance of Jesus, nothing of the fantastic as was common
in apocalyptic literature. The disciples simply perceive that Jesus
is there, and Jesus shows them the signs of his passion.

> On the evening of that day, the first day of the week, the
> doors being shut where the disciples were, for fear of the
> Jews, Jesus came and stood among them and said to them,
> "Peace be with you." When he had said this, he showed
> them his hands and his side. Then the disciples were glad
> when they saw the Lord. Jesus said to them again, "Peace
> be with you. As the Father has sent me, even so I send you."
> And when he had said this, he breathed on them, and said
> to them, "Receive the Holy Spirit. If you forgive the sins of
> any, they are forgiven; if you retain the sins of any, they are
> retained" (Jn 20:19–23).

John mentions Jesus' side because of what he had written in
19:34: "But one of the soldiers pierced his side with a spear, and
at once there came out blood and water." For John, the open side
of Jesus represented the Eucharist.

Jesus wishes them peace. We have an abrupt change from
sorrow and fear to peace, joy, and security—a change characteristic of all the Easter narratives. Jesus also gives the disciples
their mission, but only in dependence upon his own mission: "As
the Father has sent me, I also send you." The disciples are united
and joined to the unique mission of Jesus, which was given to
him by the Father. We see this enunciated earlier in the prayer
of Jesus: "Sanctify them in truth; your word is truth. As you have
sent me into the world, so I have sent them into the world. And

for their sake I consecrate myself that they also may be consecrated in your truth" (Jn 17:17–19).

The mission belongs to Christ alone. This mission implies the gift of the Holy Spirit. Matthew had promised that Jesus would be with the disciples all days (28:20), and Luke promises the Holy Spirit so that they can perform their task (Lk 24:49). However, in John, it is Christ himself who gives the Spirit: "He breathed on them and said, 'Receive the Holy Spirit' " (20:22). The word "to breathe" is infrequently used in the Bible; we can find it in the first chapter of Genesis at the creation. No doubt, John recalls that passage from Genesis to note the new creation in Christ. The result of this will be the forgiveness of sins (20:23), the result of the passion, death, and resurrection of Jesus. The destruction of the world of sin marks the beginning of the new world of the spirit. The work of the disciples by the power of the Spirit will bring this new creation to completion.

The second appearance of Jesus occurs in Jn 20:24–29:

> Now, Thomas, one of the twelve, called the twin, was not with them when Jesus came. So the other disciples told him, "We have seen the Lord." But he said to them, "Unless I see in his hands the fruit of the nails, and place my finger in the mark of the nails, and place my hand in his side, I will not believe."

> Eight days later, his disciples were again in the house, and Thomas was with them. The doors were shut but Jesus came and stood among them, and said, "Peace be with you." Then he said to Thomas, "Put your finger here and see my hands; and put out your hand, and place it in my side; do not be faithless, but believing." Thomas answered him, "My Lord and my God!" Jesus said to him, "Have you believed because you have seen me? Blessed are those who have not seen and yet believe."

The perspective here is different from that of the other appearance of Jesus. It aims at stating directly the reality of the resurrection and the difficulties in believing in it. Thomas expresses clearly the difficulty in believing in such an event. He refuses to accept the testimony of the other eleven, and he imposes conditions for his belief. Then Thomas actually sees Christ, and a new idea appears: the wounds of the passion are present in the risen body of Jesus. When he sees them, Thomas no longer wants to fulfill his conditions for belief. Instead, he gives a beautiful confession of faith: "My Lord and my God!" Christ emphasizes that we must encounter him in faith: "Blessed are those who have not seen and have believed." Peter repeats it in his epistle: "Without having seen him you love him; though you rejoice with unutterable and exalted joy. As the outcome of your faith you obtain the salvation of your souls" (1 Pet 1:8–9).

8

The Resurrection and Mystical Experience

One of the frequent charges made against the reality of the resurrection of Jesus is that, although it seems that the witness of the disciples to this event is sincere (the simplicity of the narratives shows this as well as the fact that the apostles sealed this witness with their lives), this whole experience can be explained by individual and communal mystical experience of the living Jesus. This is perhaps the hardest charge of all to attempt to refute, precisely because it is so subjective and difficult to control.

Recent theories to explain the resurrection of Jesus (e.g., Schonfield's *The Passover Plot*) are nothing more than embellishments of former theories which have long since been discredited. The fact that they are today sensational and put between slick covers does not change this. The very simplicity of the Paschal narratives in the Gospels is ample proof that the disciples were convinced that Jesus died and rose; they "saw" him, "ate" with him, "touched" him—all these words are used by the evangelists to express the concrete nature of their experience. It seems more difficult, however, to answer the charge that the disciples were deluded into a form of individual and communal mystical experiences of the living Christ by meditating on his

---

* Hugh J. Schonfield, *The Passover Plot* (New York: Bernard Geis, 1966).

words and works.

It is evident that, since the resurrection was a unique and astounding event, it would be difficult for the disciples to translate this unique experience into words comprehensible to their contemporaries. Indeed, it simply cannot be shown historically that the resurrection ever occurred. Since it was a unique event, there exists no historical probability for its enactment. The only evidence we have is the witness of the disciples of Jesus, who claim that they saw Jesus and saw that he was fully alive—but in a different state—after his humiliating death on the cross. Therefore, it must be from their witness that we establish the reasonableness of what they say. In particular, the language and expressions which they use to describe the Paschal appearances of Jesus are both simple and nonvisionary; that is, the evangelists deliberately avoid language and expressions associated with mystical experience and visionary description. This is important. We shall see that, whatever else can be said of the witness of the disciples, it cannot be said that they considered the post-Paschal encounters of Jesus in their midst to be either mystical or visionary experiences.

The Gospel Accounts of the Risen Lord

The individual appearances of Jesus are presented to various people in each of the evangelical accounts of the resurrection. Matthew mentions one to Mary Magdalene and Mary the mother of James and Salome while they are returning from the tomb (28:9–10); John also reports this appearance (20:11–18), as does Mark (16:9–11); Luke gives a manifestation of the risen Christ to two disciples on their way to Emmaus (24:13–35), to which the author of Mark 16:9–20 refers. Each of these appearances makes clear the theological preoccupation of the evangelists, as well as their apologetical attempts to reply to the difficulties of those who heard the preaching of the early Church. The evangelists did not create these appearances; they developed them, theologically, emphasizing and developing what was to their advantage. The extreme simplicity of the narration shows this clearly. The listeners of the early preaching naturally asked whether or not it was some form of ghost or phantom. The early preachers in the Chruch replied that what they had seen, felt, touched, and heard was a reality, not a phantom.

In studying the texts of the resurrection, we note some differences in the narratives concerning the risen Christ (for example, appearances in Galilee as opposed to appearances in Jerusalem). On the one hand, there is the danger of attempting to synthesize them into one perfect story or narration, to make them all agree. This is not possible nor is it desirable since the evangelists themselves did not consider it necessary to make everything agree. On the other hand, there is the opposite danger, namely, that since there are differences among the four Gospels, we can know nothing for certain.

All the Gospel accounts of the resurrection are in fundamental agreement regarding the essential facts of the death and resurrection of Jesus. Any human testimony about the same event will have some divergencies, and since the resurrection was so extraordinary an event, it is no wonder that there should be such divergencies. To have a truly objective witness, you must take him out of that experience. A living witness speaks with passion and intensity but does not see everything and usually develops his original experience by later reflection.

In the Gospels we are evidently faced with an extraordinary experience by those who saw it. To see a person return from the dead would necessarily be overwhelming. No fully objective, precise description of this event could even be possible. All the Gospels have the same original and fundamental facts about the resurrection, but on the periphery there are differences.

With such an event and its development, we can expect to find—as indeed in the case of all ancient literature when it relates the astonishing and the marvelous—an apocalyptic development. This is totally absent from the Gospel narratives, and this absence of the marvelous leads us to believe in their authenticity.

They are simple and to the point, with none of the embellishments of the extraordinary which are so common in ancient texts relating to miracle literature. The evangelists say simply that "he came" and that "he stood among them." The only other element we have in the evangelists' solicitude to relate the reality of the risen Christ is that the disciples touched Jesus and ate with him. Simplicity characterizes all of the Easter narratives.

However, there is some theological reflection manifested in these texts of the Paschal event. The fundamentals always remain the same, but in each Gospel they are developed in a slightly different theological approach. The evangelical accounts all agree that the immediate consequence of the resurrection is the universal mission of the disciples, which will be accomplished by the power of the Spirit of Jesus. This is the common structure of the Gospels. All of the texts reveal these two chief characteristics.

Distinctions between Mystical and Ordinary Events

We have seen how the disciples emphasized the fact of their having seen the risen Christ. These events are described for us in a clear, simple, and sober way. The Gospels express a concreteness of vocabulary ("eat," "touch," "see") with the result that we know that the experiences of the disciples were not some form of phantom or vision. Yet could the disciples really distinguish between a mystical experience and the experience of Easter? This question has troubled the minds of Christian thinkers for centuries.

The Old Testament clearly distinguishes mystical experiences from ordinary human experiences. The former are mostly imaginary. Amos relates a vision concerning the condition and future of Israel: "The words of Amos, who was among the shepherds of Tekoa, which he saw concerning Israel . . . " (1:1). Still later, Amos says: "He showed me. Behold, the Lord was standing beside a wall built with a plumb line, with a plumb line in his

hand. And the Lord said to me, 'Amos, what do you see?' "
(7:7–8). Jeremiah also records visions for us in his prophecies: the
rod of almond (1:11), the boiling pot (1:13), , and others. Many
times a vision serves as a vehicle for discovering a divine meaning in connection with some ordinary event of everyday life.

There are also some visions in the book of Genesis. In Gen
15:1–17 we are told of a vision which Abraham had when the Lord
made a covenant with him: "After these things the word of the
Lord came to Abraham in a vision, 'Fear not, Abram, I am your
shield.' " The text describes a sort of psychological state of
Abraham in which he is outside the realm of ordinary human
experience and in which he perceives a divine presence.

Isaiah also had a vision in which he was summoned to his
mission: "In the year that King Ozziah died I saw the Lord
sitting upon a throne, high and lifted up; and his train filled the
room" (6:1). One of the Seraphim purifies his lips with a burning
coal to prepare him for his mission. These are only a few exam-
ples of the forms of visions which characterize the Old Testament. There are two possible explanations.

It is possible that the mystical experience which the prophet
lives—the profound perception of the reality of God which takes
place in the depth of his personal reality—is beyond the grasp
of his own personality, intelligence, and imagination. At the
same time, his imagination is moved so that the prophet tries to
communicate the ineffable by means of images. Thus the essential point here is not the words themselves but the reality sym-
bolized by these images (this was the view of Thomas Aquinas).

There is another possible explanation of these events. The
Old Testament continuously presents us with images for describing the reality of God: "Hear, you peoples, all of you; harken,
oh earth, and all that is in it; and let the Lord God be a witness
against you, the Lord from his holy temple. For behold the Lord
is coming forth out of his place, and will come down and tread
upon the high places of the earth. And the mountains will melt
under him and the valleys will be cleft, like wax before the fire,
like waters poured down a steep place" (Micah 1:2–4). This very

early way of describing God and his actions was passed on to the other prophets and found its final expression in the book of Revelation. This vocabulary was thus used to describe God, and tradition took it up and used it.

The writers of the New Testament also have a language to describe mystical experience; but it is extremely important to realize that this language differs notably from that used to describe the risen Christ. As an example, we have the description of St. Paul concerning his vision on the way to Damascus: "I know a man in Christ who fourteen years ago was caught up to the third heaven— whether in the body or out of the body I do not know, God knows. And I know that this man was caught up into Paradise—whether in the body or out of the body I do not know, God knows—and he heard things which cannot be told, which man may not utter" (2 Cor 12:2–4). The words which Paul uses: "in the body," "caught up," "third heaven"—are all a description of Paul caught up in a vision. His vision was so intense that he has no way to communicate it to other human beings ("which man may not utter").

Paul is not the only person in the New Testament to have visions or a mystical experience. Acts 7:30–34 recalls the vision of the burning bush of Moses (cf. Ex 3:1–10). In this text, the verb form of the technical word for "vision" *(horama)* is used: "Now when forty years had passed, an angel appeared [*ophthē*] to him in the wilderness of Mount Sinai, in a flame of fire in a bush."

Acts 9:10 reports the vision of Ananias, in which the technical Greek word *horama* is used: "Now there was a disciple at Damascus named Ananias. The Lord said to him in a vision [*en horamati*]. . . ." Acts 10:3–6 relates the vision of the centurion Cornelius, and "in a vision" *(en horamati)* appears again (10:3). Peter has a vision expressed in the picture of a sheet filled with all sorts of animals coming down from heaven: "Now Peter was inwardly perplexed as to what the vision [*to horama*] which he had seen might mean" (10:17). One may see the same word used in Acts 11:5; 12:9; 16:9–10; and 18:9. Along with the word *horama*, another word is also used: "He fell into a trance" *(ekstasis,* Acts

10:10). We see this again in 11:5: "I was in the city of Joppa praying; and in a trance [*ekstasi*]. I saw a vision [*horama*]." The Greek word *ekstasis* means "being out of oneself" in a sort of extraordinary psychological state which cuts a person off from his normal intellectual and sensory perception. Paul explicitly refers to this phenomenon as having happened to him while he was praying in the temple (Acts 22:17).

The Gospels of Mark and Luke also mention the phenomenon of a person "being out of himself." "And immediately they were overcome with amazement" *(ekestesan)* Mk 5:42). "And they went out and fled from the tomb; for trembling and astonishment [*ekstasis*] had come upon them" (Mk 16:8). "And amazement [*ekstasis*] seized them all . . ." (Lk 5:26).

The only time we find the word *ekstasis* in the context of the resurrection is in Mk 16:8, but it does not refer to an appearance by Jesus but to the fear of the women who came to the tomb.

Matthew also gives messages in dreams, for instance, the vision which Joseph has to take Mary as his wife (Mt 1:20-23), the vision of the Magi (2:12), and the vision warning Joseph to flee with the holy family (2:13). We find another example of dream or vision in Mt 27:19, where Pilate's wife tries to warn him during the passion of Jesus.

Thus both the personages of the Old as well as of the New Testament are well acquainted with mystical experiences in which they perceived the reality of God. Around this was developed a whole vocabulary. Yet the disciples *never* used this vocabulary when describing the appearances of Jesus. Their language is simple; for example, "he stood in the midst of them" and "they saw him." The disciples avoid all apocalyptic, mystic, or visionary language when describing the risen Christ. Some such language is used by the evangelists to describe the messenger or messengers at the tomb (cf. Mk 16:1-8; Mt 28:1-8; Lk 24:1-11) but never to describe the risen Christ.

When the Gospels describe the appearances of Jesus and the reaction of the disciples at the encounter, they pass from fear to joy. The words *horama* or *ekstasis* never appear in this context. The evangelists describe the disciples as being in the presence of someone like themselves. Luke directly attests to the fact that Jesus is not a spirit, and therefore this cannot be a mystical experience perceived through the imagination. The disciples see Jesus, they touch him and eat with him (Lk 24:36–43). Moreover, Jesus appeared to many at the same time, and there is no mystical experience on record where we have a properly collective mystical experience. These appearances of Jesus were limited to a specific period of time. Divine charisms were experienced in the early Church many times (cf. 1 Cor 12:1–12) but not another experience of the risen Jesus. In Acts 1:3 Luke says that Jesus appeared to the disciples for a period of forty days after the resurrection. Mark, Matthew, and John are not so specific. After a short time we do know that it took place and that soon these appearances ceased completely.

The resurrection, therefore, was not really a scientific event. Yet it was historical. It was unique and irreducible to anything else that the apostles testify as having seen. Jesus is not in the empty tomb (the negative sign of the resurrection), but there is the positive indication of the witness of the apostles that they had seen Jesus alive, even if Jesus had not simply returned to his former life and condition. The very simplicity of their language and description is a strong indication of the veracity of the event.

The resurrection is the starting point of all Christian thinking, of the Christian reality itself:

> If Christ has not been raised, then our preaching is in vain and your faith is in vain. We are even found to be misrepresenting God, because we testified of God that he raised Christ. . . . If Christ has not been raised, your faith is futile and you are still in your sins. Then those who have also fallen asleep in Christ have perished. If for this life only we have hoped in Christ, we are of all men most to be pitied" (1 Cor 15:14–15, 17–19).

Thus the sober testimony of the apostles with regard to the resurrection of Jesus assures us of its authenticity. Nothing could have prepared the apostles for this unique experience. Today—as in all ages past—we can only accept or reject this simple testimony of the apostles. The resurrection is and remains a mystery which we cannot fully grasp. Whoever denies it must give an explanation. The explanation that the resurrection was a visionary or mystical experience is ruled out by the evangelical texts themselves. The testimony of the Gospels that the resurrection is a fact is the only satisfactory explanation capable of accounting for the faith of Christians from apostolic times to the present.

Selected Bibliography

BARRETT, C. K., *Jesus and the Gospel Tradition*. Nashville: John Knox Press, 1967.

BENOIT, P., *The Passion and Resurrection of the Lord*. New York: Herder & Herder, 1969.

BROWN, R., *Jesus: God and Man*. Milwaukee: The Bruce Publishing Company, 1967.

————, "The Resurrection and Biblical Criticism," *Commonweal Papers #2: Jesus (Commonweal*, November 24, 1967), 232–236. Reprinted in *God, Jesus and The Spirit*, ed. Daniel J. Callahan. New York: Herder and Herder, 1969.

CERFAUX, L., *The Christian in the Theology of Saint Paul*. New York: Herder & Herder, 1967.

DURWELL, F. X., *The Resurrection*. New York: Sheed & Ward, 1964.

JEREMIAS, J., *The Problem of the Historical Jesus*. Philadelphia: The Fortress Press, 1966.

LÉON-DUFOUR, X., *The Gospels and the Jesus of History*. New York: Desclee, 1968.

MICHL, J., *Questions about Jesus*. Milwaukee: The Bruce Publishing Company, 1969.

NIEBUHR, R. H., *Resurrection and Historical Reason*. New York: Charles Scribner's Sons, 1957.

RAHNER, K., *Everyday Faith*. New York: Herder & Herder, 1967.

RAMSEY, A. M., *The Resurrection of Christ.* London: Geoffrey Bles, 1965.

STANLEY, D. M., *Christ's Resurrection in Pauline Soteriology.* Rome: Pontifical Biblical Institute, 1961.

Who Is Jesus of Nazareth?, Volume II of *Concilium.* Glen Rock, N.J.: The Paulist Press, 1966.